# Seniors

## Guide to
# Android

# Welcome

An Android phone is one of the most useful pieces of technology you can buy. Not only can it make phone calls for you, but it can also browse the web, video call friends and family, capture amazing photos, and even translate languages.

The best thing about Android, however, is that it's so easy to use. You can never do the wrong thing, as the Home screen is just a swipe of your finger away; and if you're ever unsure what to do, then you can simply ask Google Assistant -- a digital aide that can answer nearly any question.

This brand new book for 2022 is all about making sense of Android smartphones, even if you've never used one before. You'll learn about the very basics, how the built-in apps work, and how you can use an Android device to enrich and improve your life. Large images and step-by-step guides are used throughout to help you along the way.

As you become more familiar with Android and its apps, you might have specific questions that aren't covered in this book. If so, feel free to send me an email at tom@leafpublishing.co.uk, and I'll be more than happy to help.

**Tom Rudderham**
**Author**
tom@leafpublishing.co.uk

## Credits:

**Author:** Tom Rudderham
**Editor:** Zeljko Jurancevic
**Copy Editor:** Caroline Denham

**Published by:**
Leaf Publishing LTD
www.leafpublishing.co.uk

**ISBN:** 9798356774829

# Contents

## Welcome

**12**
Learn about accessories

## Setting Up

**21**
Access Quick Settings

## The Basics

**40**
Talk to Google Assistant

## Apps

**50**
Discover apps on your phone

# Web & Communication

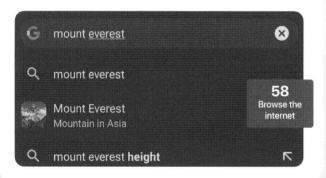

# Maps, Notes, & Utilities

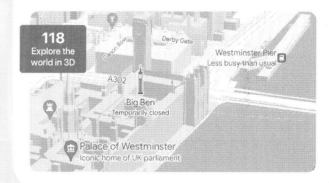

# Camera & Photos

# Settings & Troubleshooting

# Entertainment & News

# Terminology

## Wondering what all those words and phrases mean?

Every Android phone is a rather complicated piece of equipment, so perhaps it's inevitable that talking about it involves using a wide-ranging assortment of words, phrases, and terminology. In this book, you're going to hear a lot about Android hardware, software, and features. Don't worry, each one of them will be explained as we go, so you'll never feel confused or get lost halfway through a paragraph. To get you started, here are a few of the words we will be using constantly throughout this book...

### Android

This is the name of the software which powers your phone. It's made by Google, and is one of the most complicated pieces of software ever created by man. It tells your phone how to turn on, how to take a photo, how to browse the internet, how to scan your fingerprint, plus so much more. It can also learn over time. Android will learn about your habits, how you type to individual people, where you travel, what you look like and what you sound like. It uses all of this learning to help you type quicker, find photos quicker, and basically use your phone in a more efficient manner.

When most people think of the word Android, they imagine the home screen of their phone, the place where all the icons are, which let you open the internet browser or email application. You can think of it like that too, but really, it's so much more.

### App

The word app is short for application. An application is a piece of software, separate from Android, which lets you do something. There's an app on your phone for taking a picture. There's an app for sending messages. There's an app for looking at your photos. I'm sure you get the idea.

### Google Play Store

This is the app you open to find additional apps, games, books, and media. Think of Google Play as a vast market for all of these things. You can find the Google Play app on your Android phone. It has a colourful triangle on its side.

### Browser

This is the term used to describe an app for navigating the internet. On an Android phone, the "browser "is called Chrome, but there are other browsers available to install from the App Store, such as Firefox and Microsoft Edge.

### Home Screen

The Home Screen is where you'll find all the apps installed on your phone, plus a search box that takes you straight to Google. The Home Screen is the first place you see after unlocking your phone, and every time you close an app you'll return to the Home Screen.

## Settings

You can heavily configure how your Android phone notifies you of new messages, how bright the screen is, how loud the speakers are, and even how apps track your location. These configurations are called "settings', and to make any of these changes (plus much more), then you need to open the Settings app.

## Gestures

When we talk about gestures on a smartphone, we're referring to the use of your fingers to initiate an action. Let's say you want to zoom into a photo. The gesture to do this would be to place two fingers on the screen then move them apart. You can find out more about gestures by visting page **10**.

## Encryption

Think of encryption as a padlock for words, but instead of 0-9 on the padlock, it's A-Z, plus 0-9. The software on your phone uses encryption all the time. Whenever you send a message to a friend, all the letters you type are scrambled up, sent to the other person, then de-scrambled on their phone. The same goes for video calls you make, your credit cards details when you check out on the internet, and much more. Nearly everything you do on your phone is encrypted, which is why even the FBI can't access your phone without your password or biometric information.

## Sleep

You can put your phone to sleep by pressing the power button. When it's asleep, it will still check for new messages, emails, and notifications, but the screen will be turned off, and it won't use much power. In sleep mode, your phone can last for nearly a week on a full battery charge, while in normal use (when the screen is on), it's more like 10 hours.

## Storage

Your Android phone comes with a limited amount of space for storing photos, videos, apps, and other content. When you bought your phone, you needed to choose how much storage it had available, and the more storage space you chose, the more expensive it was to buy.

## Icon

The small image that represents an app is usually referred to as an "icon". It's basically a small image that when tapped on, let's you open an app, or initiate an action.

### Don't understand another term?

Feel free to email Tom, the author of this book at tom@leafpublishing.co.uk, and he'll be happy to explain any further terms or phrases that you're unsure about.

# Things to keep in mind

## Android phones are easier to use than you might think...

Whether you've just bought your new smartphone, or been given one by a friend or family member, there are a few things to keep in mind.

## You do everything with just your fingertip

When you want to open an app, make a picture bigger, or scroll through a page, all you need to do is tap on the screen with your fingertip. Touch screens work by detecting the static electricity from your finger, so you don't need to press hard. A light tap will work. Keep in mind that fingernails don't transmit static, only skin, so if you have long fingernails, try tapping with the soft part of your finger.

## You can never do the wrong thing

You'll never break your phone by opening the wrong app, or by tapping on the wrong button, so don't worry about making a mistake. Most apps have sensible names, so if you want to send a message, open the Messages app, and if you want to look at photos, tap on the Photos app.

If you're unsure about an app, feel free to open it anyway, you can always go back by swiping your finger upwards from the very bottom of the screen to the top. If you have an older Android phone, then you can also press the Home button at the bottom of the screen. Here's how it looks:

| Android v 5 - 11 | Android v 1 - 4 | Samsung |
|:---:|:---:|:---:|
| ◯ | ⌂ | ☐ |

## You can talk to your phone

Your phone has a built-in assistant called Google Assistant (covered in more detail on page **39**). You can use Google Assistant to do basic things like make a phone call, perform simple maths, or set a timer. To do this, either press and hold on the power button, or say "OK Google" out-loud, then say something like "call Joe", "remind me to take the dinner out of the oven in 10 minutes", or "what's 15 times 30?". After a moment or two, Google Assistant will perform your request.

# Android phones come in many shapes and sizes

There are a lot of smartphones available. Some fit in one hand and are quite affordable, while others are the size of small pocketbooks and are less affordable. They're also made from different materials. Some are entirely plastic, while others feature brushed metal frames. You might also notice differences around the back, with some Android phones featuring just a single camera lens, while others have multiple lenses protruding out of the back.

# There are many versions of the Android operating system

Turn on any Android phone and you'll quickly notice that the buttons, background wallpapers, and colours look different to other Android phones. That's because the Android operating system is highly customisable. This enables manufacturers of Android phones to tweak the look and layout of their phones, helping them to stand out from the crowd. It also means you can tweak your own phone to suit your tastes and needs.

However, this might cause some confusion if you're going from one phone to another, as an app might have moved place, or an important button might be a different shape (see back across the page for an example of how the Home button can change shape). It might also mean that the phone you hold in your hand looks different to the phones used to make this book. If that's the case, don't worry, as all Android phones can be used in nearly identical ways. You'll always be able to find your apps in the same way, search for things in the same way, and browse the web in the same way. It just might look a little different from one device to another.

**Pixel Home Screen**

**Samsung Home Screen**

**Android v4 Home Screen**

# How to choose a phone

A few tips to help you buy the right phone for you...

At the time of writing, during the early months of 2022, there are more than 1,500 different makes and models of Android phones. Some have incredible cameras, others have massive touchscreens, while a few are designed to be as affordable as possible. If you haven't already purchased an Android phone, then here are some tips to help you choose the right model...

## Size

All Android phones are fairly large, but if you're concerned about size, then look for a smaller model. The Asus Zenfone 8 is a good choice, as is the Google Pixel 4a.

## Cost

The cost of buying a new smartphone has slowly risen year by year over the last decade, but you can often buy last year's model at a discount. Head into your local electronics store, see what the latest phone is (for example, the Pixel 6), then ask about last years model (for example, the Pixel 5).

## Camera

All Android phones include cameras around the back. If taking sharp photos is important for you, then make a note of the total megapixel count. The higher the number, the sharper the image. Anything above 12 megapixels is a good start, but keep in mind that once you reach astronomical figures, any photos taken in low-light might appear grainy and dark. You should also make sure the phone has a flash on the back, as this will enable you to take great photos of people at night.

## Version of Android

It's a good idea to buy a phone that has the default, stock version of Google's Android operating system installed. Many manufacturers, such as Samsung, have their own customised version of Android. While this can offer additional features and apps, you'll often miss out on important security updates from Google. Phone's which offer the default, unaltered version of Android include the Google Pixel 4, 4a, 5, 6, and 6 Pro. From Nokia you'll find the Nokia 5.4, 8.3, and X family.

## Apps

If you decide to buy a phone that doesn't run the stock version of Android, make sure it can run the Google Play Store. This app enables you to download third-party apps (such as Facebook and WhatsApp). Some bargain phones prevent you from running apps not provided by the manufacturer.

# How to use a touchscreen

The basics of tapping, swiping, and pinching...

As the proud owner of a new Android phone, you might have noticed the vast screen that takes up the front of the device. Nearly everything you do with a smartphone is performed via this screen. Usually, a gentle tap of your fingertip is all it takes to open an app or press a button, but over time a small number of gestures have been invented to let you perform more complex tasks.

Before we get around to setting up your new phone, let's go over these gestures to make sure you know the difference between a tap and a swipe.

## Tap

This is the most basic gesture you can perform. All you need to do is lightly tap on something on the touchscreen (such as an app or picture), and it will react to your touch.

## Tap and hold

You can often access additional options by placing your finger on something and then keeping it there. After a moment or two, you'll see a secondary menu appear below your finger.

## Double tap

You can often get a closer look at something by quickly tapping twice on top of it. For example, if you tap twice on a photo it will zoom in.

## Swipe

This describes the action of placing your finger on the screen, then sliding it to another location. To give an example, you can often go back to an earlier page by sliding your finger from left to right.

## Scroll

This is a term used to describe moving up or down through a page or document. To scroll the page, simply place your finger on the screen and then slide it upwards.

## Drag

If you tap and hold on something (such as an app), you can then move it somewhere else by dragging it with your finger. This helpful gesture will let you rearrange the apps on the Home Screen.

## Pinch

You can zoom into photos, web pages, and documents by placing two fingers onto the screen and then moving them apart. Similarly, you can zoom out by placing two fingers on the screen and then moving them inwards.

## Rotate

If you want to rotate a photo or object on the screen, place two fingers on top of it and rotate them one way or another.

# Accessories

## Protect your new phone, find a vehicle mount, and much more...

Android phones aren't exactly cheap, especially the high-end models which include multiple cameras and vast touchscreens. This means that you might want to invest in a fashionable protective case and maybe even a mount so you can use your phone while driving. The Android phone accessory market is vast and catered for each device, but here are some of the essentials that you can expect to find...

## Protective Cases

These come in a variety of materials and colours. If you don't want to add bulk to your phone, then look for a "slim" case that's light and thin. If you prefer to customise your phone with colour and detail, then look for a patterned case. Some of the more expensive cases might offer protection from heavy forces (think a car rolling over the phone), while others are more fashionable and sparkly.

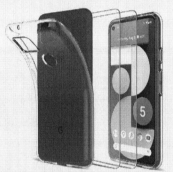
*LK Case*

*Ringke Fusion*

*Spigen Liquid Air Case*

*Mikikit Silicone Case*

## Headphones

If you're planning to listen to music or media through your phone, then a good pair of headphones is essential. The latest Android phones don't have a headphone socket, so look for a great set of wireless Bluetooth headphones. Here are a few suggestions:

*ACAGET USB C*
*Headphones*

*Cambridge Audio*
*Melomania*

*Yamaha YH-E700A*

*Yamaha TW-E3A*

# Screen Protectors

A clear plastic film that adheres to the touchscreen, screen protectors are designed to prevent the glass screen from being scratched by sharp objects (such as keys in your pocket). If you purchase a screen protector for your phone, make sure it's designed specifically for your device, as all Android phones are slightly different in size.

# Vehicle mount

If you take your phone into the car to play music, answer calls, or control the screen using Android Auto, then a good vehicle mount is an essential purchase. It will enable you to safely see your phone's screen while driving, although please be aware that the laws for using a phone whilst driving differ from country to country, and in the United States, from state to state.

*VANMASS Car Phone Holder Mount*

*Kensington Windscreen and Vent Car Mount*

*Cinati Car Phone Holder*

# Wireless charger

Not all Android phones can charge wirelessly, but if yours supports this feature, then a wireless charger makes for a convieniant way to charge your phone each night. All you need to do is place the phone on the charging mat, and it will immediately start to charge. The only downside to wireless charging is speed; expect your phone to take anywhere between 2-4x more time to charge when compared to using a USB/C cable.

# Battery pack

A battery back is a good investment if you plan to be away from a plug socket for some time, such as when you're on a camping trip or staying overnight in a hotel. A typical battery pack can re-charge your phone one or two times, and they're portable too, being small enough to fit into a backpack or purse.

# Android hardware

## An exploration of the hardware features typically found on each Android phone...

All Android phones have one thing in common: a huge touchscreen on the front of the device. Depending on the manufacturer, you might also find a front-facing camera, multiple speakers, a power button, and volume buttons. Here's an overview of each feature and button that you can expect to find...

## Front:

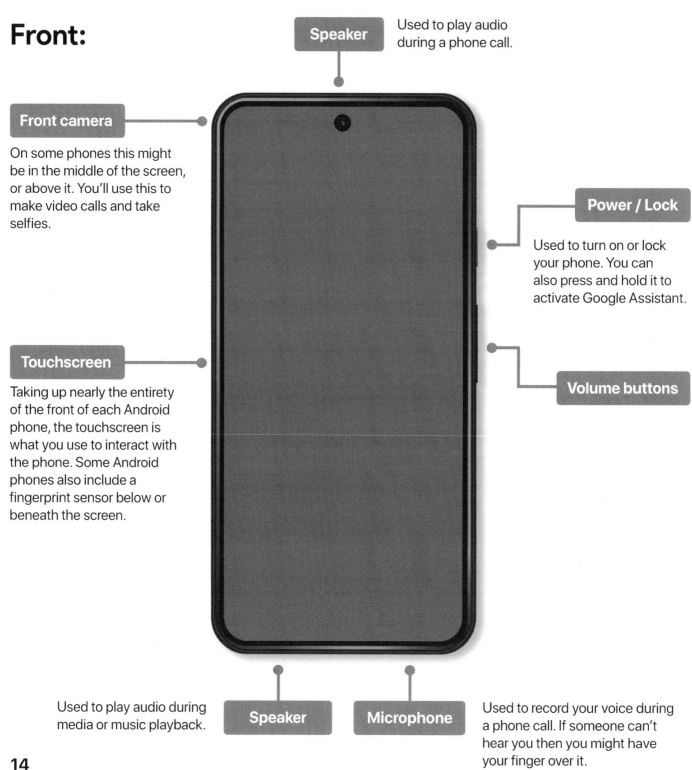

**Speaker**
Used to play audio during a phone call.

**Front camera**
On some phones this might be in the middle of the screen, or above it. You'll use this to make video calls and take selfies.

**Power / Lock**
Used to turn on or lock your phone. You can also press and hold it to activate Google Assistant.

**Touchscreen**
Taking up nearly the entirety of the front of each Android phone, the touchscreen is what you use to interact with the phone. Some Android phones also include a fingerprint sensor below or beneath the screen.

**Volume buttons**

Used to play audio during media or music playback.

**Speaker**

**Microphone**
Used to record your voice during a phone call. If someone can't hear you then you might have your finger over it.

# Back:

**Rear camera**

Used to take photos and videos. Some Android phones have multiple lenses, with the secondary lenses used for telescopic or macro photos.

**LED Flash**

This bright spot on the rear camera is used as either the camera flash, or as a flashlight/torch.

**Fingerprint sensor**

Some Android phones include a fingerprint sensor for unlocking the device. On the latest phones this might be underneath the touchscreen or on the front of the phone.

Charge your phone or connect it to a computer.

**USB / Power port**

# Setup your brand new Android

## It's time to get going with your new phone...

Unless you've been given an Android phone as a hand-me-down from a loved one, your first experience with an Android phone will be to take it out of the box. Savour the moment, because the phone will never be as squeaky clean and fresh as it is in this very first moment. Dig around in the box and you'll find the following things:

- **The phone itself.** Likely wrapped in a plastic or paper film, which you can carefully peel off and discard.
- **A USB charging cable.** You can plug this cable into a wall adaptor (perhaps included in the box), a computer, or any other device with a USB socket to charge your phone.
- **A useless pamphlet.** It might be a few pages long, and it might be about the size of a credit card. Typically you'll find safety information and warranty details inside.
- **A SIM card removal tool.** It might look like a toothpick. You can use this to pop the SIM card tray open on the side of your phone.
- **Other paraphernalia**. Depending on how generous the phone's manufacturer is, you might find free headphones, stickers, and adaptors.

## 1 Insert a SIM card

Think of a SIM card as the thing which lets your Android make phone calls and browse the internet. It also stores your phone number, so if you take your SIM card and put it into another phone, you transfer the number across devices. Sometimes the sales staff in a store will insert the SIM card for you, but it's really not difficult to do. Here's how it works:

- Insert the pointy end of the SIM tray tool into the small hole on the side of your phone. Press hard, and the SIM tray will pop out slightly.
- Carefully place your SIM card into the SIM tray. You might have to flip it around to make sure it fits properly. If your SIM card is too big, then you can usually break the edges off to make it smaller (don't worry, SIM cards are designed to be used in a number of SIM tray sizes).
- Slide the SIM tray back into your phone and you're good to go.

## 2 Power up your new phone

To do this, press and hold the **Power** button. You might have to hold down the button for a few seconds before the screen lights up.

## ③ Answer a *lot* of questions

Your new phone wants to know all about you. It wants to know what language you speak, what the Wi-Fi details are, the local time zone, and if your phone has a fingerprint sensor, your fingerprint details. This will let you unlock your phone by placing your fingertip on the screen (or a fingerprint sensor around the back).

## ④ Sign into your Google account

At some point during the setup process, your new phone will ask you to sign in to a Google account. This lets your phone learn all of your contacts, your calendar events, add your email account, and even copy across any photos you have taken with a previous Android.

If you don't have a Google account yet, then you can create one on the spot by tapping the **Create account** button.

Alternatively, you can skip this step and add a Google account at a later date (or not add one at all, it's up to you).

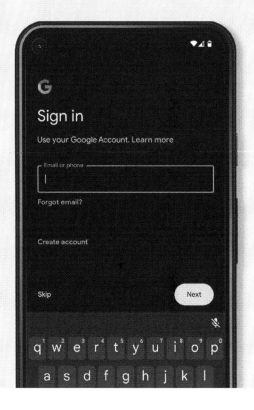

Once you have followed all the setup steps and logged into your Google account, then your phone will be ready to use. Here are some things to keep in mind as you open apps for the first time:

- You don't need to use any of the apps pre-installed by the manufacturer of your phone. Similarly, you don't have to create an account for your phone's manufacturer to use it.

- Some apps might ask permission to know your current location. It's okay to agree to this, as there are many benefits to letting your phone and its apps know where you are. For example, a weather app might be able to let you know when it's about to rain, while the Maps app can give you directions around town. If you decide to change your mind at a later time, then you can adjust or disable permissions from the Settings app.

- As with your location, some apps might ask for your permission to access the camera or your phone contacts. Facebook, for example, will look at your contacts list and suggest friends that you can add, while Whatsapp will let you send a photo or video to someone else. It's usually okay to agree to this permission. Go with your gut feeling, and stick to well-known apps, and don't forget you can change permission settings at a later time.

# The Lock Screen

## How to unlock your phone and interact with notifications...

Tap on your phone's screen or press the **Power** button, and the Lock Screen will fade into view. From here you'll see the time and date, all of your notifications (unless the phone is in Do Not Disturb mode, see page **33** for more on that), and depending on your phone's manufacturer, shortcuts to the Camera and Phone apps.

### Notification

- To clear a notification away, swipe it left or right.
- To interact with a notification, simply tap on it.

### Fingerprint sensor

If your phone has a fingerprint sensor under the screen, just place your finger (or thumb) over the button to unlock your phone. Some Android phones have a sensor around the back, while others will ask for a PIN code instead.

### Unlock

Swipe upwards to unlock your phone. If you have an older device, press the Home button instead. Here's how it looks on a number of devices:

# The Home Screen

## The place where your favourite apps live...

Get past the Lock Screen and the first thing you'll see is the Home Screen. Think of it as the default place where you visit every time you unlock your phone or close an app. From the Home Screen you can find your favourite apps, and a search bar that takes you straight to Google.

**Wallpaper**

If you don't like the default wallpaper, **tap and hold** on it and then choose **Wallpaper & Style**.

**Default apps**

Depending on your phone's manufacturer, you'll see default apps here including YouTube, Photos, and the Play Store.

**Search bar**

This is the Google Search bar. You can tap on it to search the web, or look for apps and settings on your phone.

**Google Assistant**

Tap the **Microphone** button to open Google Assistant. You can then use your voice to ask questions and perform commands. Turn to page **39** to find out more.

**Google Lens**

Tap the **colourful square** to open Google Lens. This clever feature uses the camera to recognise obects, landmarks, and products. Turn to page **94** to find out more.

19

# The very basics

With the setup process out of the way, let's take a look at the first steps to using your Android phone...

## Powering on and off

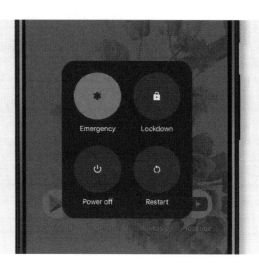

To turn on your phone, press and hold the **Power** button until the screen turns on.

To turn your phone off, hold both the **Power** button and the **volume uo** buttons. You will then see buttons for powering off or restarting your phone.

## Sleep mode

Your phone will automatically lock itself and go into sleep mode if left alone for 1 minute. While asleep it will still check for new messages, and let you know when a phone call comes through, but the screen will be turned off and it will use less power.

To put your phone to sleep straight away, press the **Power** button once.

To wake your phone up, either tap on the screen or press the **Power** button.

## Adjust sleep mode

To adjust the length of time it takes for your phone to go into sleep mode, open the **Settings** app, tap on **Display**, then tap **Screen timeout**. You can then choose from a variety of lengths before the phone goes to sleep.

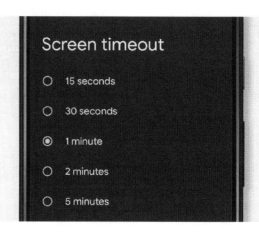

# Access Quick Settings

Think of Quick Settings as a place where you can change the screen brightness, adjust the volume, and access several other settings. You can always find it by **swiping two fingers downwards** from the very top of the screen.

# Adjust the volume

You can use the two buttons on the side of your phone to turn the volume up or down. You can also press and hold one of these buttons to quickly turn the volume to its maximum setting or mute it. To fine-tune the volume levels for media, phone calls, notifications, and alarms, tap the **options** button below the slider, then adjust the settings.

# Change the brightness

You can adjust the screen brightness in two ways. The first is to open Quick Settings, then use the brightness slider at the top. Alternatively, open the **Settings** app, tap on **Display**, then tap **Brightness level**.

# Adjust settings

If you'd like to make changes to your phone, such as the wallpaper, notification settings, Wi-Fi connection and much more, then swipe upwards from the Home screen to access all of your apps, then tap on the **Settings** app. Feel free to browse through the settings or use the search box to find something specific.

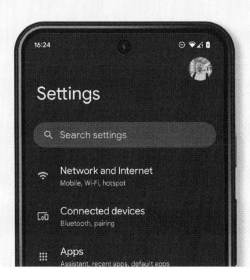

# The basics of using apps

## Learn how to open, close, and manage apps...

Take a look at your phone's screen and you'll see a number of small icons going from top to bottom. Each of these icons represents an individual app on your device. Look closely, and you'll see an app for taking photos, an app for accessing your calendar, an app for looking at Maps... the list goes on and on. On this spread of pages we'll explore how to open and close apps, delete them, and organise them into folders.

## Open an app

You can open any app on your phone by lightly tapping on its icon. Just a quick tap of your fingertip is all that's needed.

## Close an app

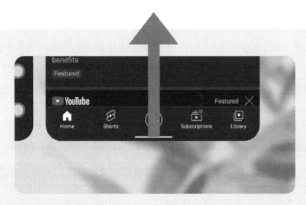

When you're ready to close an app and return to the home screen, just swipe upwards from the bottom of the screen. On older Android phones you can also press the Home button, which looks like this:

## See all the apps on your phone

There are a lot of apps included with your phone, but you can't see them all from the Home Screen. Instead, the majority of them are tucked away in the App Drawer. To find it, swipe upwards on the Home Screen. You'll then see a grid of apps appear with a search box above. Feel free to browse through the apps on your phone, or if there's a specific app you're looking for, use the search box to quickly find it.

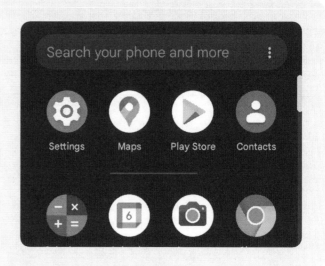

# Delete an app

If you've downloaded an app but want to remove it, simply **tap and hold** on the app icon, tap **App info**, then on the following screen choose **Uninstall**.

# Tap and hold for options

You can **tap and hold** on most things on your Android phone to access additional options, so tap and hold on an app and you can rearrange it or quickly jump to something within the app.

# Create a folder of apps

It's a good idea to group similar apps into folders. For example, you might want to move all of your social media apps into a folder called "Social". To do this, **tap and hold** on an app, then drag it on top of another app. This will create a folder of apps. You can rename a folder by tapping and holding on its name.

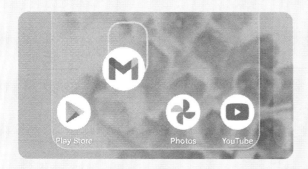

# Rearrange your apps

To move an app to another part of the screen, simply **tap and hold** on it then slide it somewhere else. As you do this you'll notice a grid appear beneath your finger. This acts as a guide, and will show you where you can "drop" the app into place.

23

# Customise the Home screen

## Change the wallpaper, adjust colours, and more...

You're going to spend a lot of time looking at the Home screen, so it's worth customising it to make it feel yours. The Home screen is surprisingly adapt, able to change not only its wallpaper, but the surrounding colours, apps, and even introduce boxes of information called widgets. We'll take a look at all of these over the next four pages.

## How to navigate Home screens

The Home screen is actually a series of screens, but you can only see one at a time. To move from one to another, swipe left and right.

On the left side you should find a series of news stories and videos based upon your interest and browsing history. You might see something different, however, depending on your phone's manufacturer.

Swipe towards the right, and you'll see a secondary Home screen, where you can add additional apps and widgets. If you can't scroll right, then you have not added any additional apps or widgets yet. To add a second screen, **tap and hold** on an existing app, then drag it to the right side of the screen. You'll see a grid appear, enabling you to keep dragging the app towards the right and onto another screen.

**The news feed.**

**Main Home screen**

**Secondary Home screen**

# Change the wallpaper

One of the easiest and most dramatic ways to customise the Home screen is to change the wallpaper. There are plenty of stock wallpapers to choose from. Some even subtly animate in the background, with rolling waves, flying birds and moving clouds. You can also use a photo of your own. To change the wallpaper:

1. **Tap and hold** on an empty space of the Home screen, then choose **Wallpaper & style**.

2. On the next screen, tap **Change wallpaper**.

3. To use a photo of your own, tap **My photos**. To browse animated wallpapers, tap **Living Universe**. Alternatively, browse the other categories further down the screen.

4. Once you've made a selection, tap the **tick** button in the lower-right corner, then choose if you want to add the new wallpaper to the Lock screen, Home screen, or both.

# Change the accent colour

The colour of buttons and text will change to match your wallpaper. This is a helpful and unique way to make each wallpaper feel different, but if you'd rather choose your own colour scheme, then:

1. **Tap and hold** on an empty space of the Home screen, then choose **Wallpaper & style**.

2. Notice the two buttons att the bottom of the Wallpaper & style panel. **Wallpaper colours** will let you pick three colour schemes based on the wallpaper image, while **Basic colours** will enable you to choose from four solid colour choices based on the wallpaper.

# Add widgets

## Add additional information to the Home screen...

Think of widgets as small windows of helpful information that you can place around the Home screen of your phone. You'll find widgets that display the latest news, widgets that display photos from your library, and even a "smart" widget, which changes throughout the day to show you helpful information.

Your phone might come with some widgets pre-installed on the Home screen. These widgets might show the weather or the remaining battery. Alternatively, your phone might not come with any widgets at all, and just show a few apps along the bottom the Home screen. However your phone looks straight out of the box, you can always add, remove, and customise widgets.

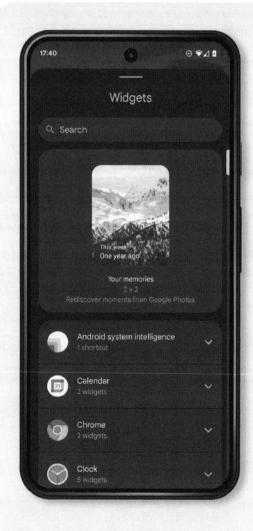

## How to browse widgets

To browse the widget library, go to the Home screen of your phone, then **tap and hold** on an empty space. When a pop-up window appears below your finger, tap **Widgets**.

At the top of the screen are suggested widgets based on your recent activity. Scroll down, and you'll find a list of every widget available. If you already know which widget you're looking for, then use the search field at the top of the window to find it.

## Notes about widgets

- You can have as many widgets on the Home screen as you like.

- You can also have a Home screen with just a single widget on it and nothing else.

- If it doesn't look like there's room on the Home screen for a widget, simply slide it to the right-side of the screen and you'll be able to place it on a secondary Home screen.

- Tap on a widget within the list, and you'll see the various sizes it's available in. Some take up the space of two app icons, while a few can be as big as four app icons.

# Add a widget

When you're ready to add a widget, **tap and hold** on it from within the widget library, and you'll see the Home screen appear. Notice there's a grid over the Home screen. This is designed to help you place the widget. Without letting go, drag the widget into place over the grid. When you're happy with its location, let go, and it will snap into place.

Some widgets require further information before they're ready. Gmail, for example, will ask you to choose an inbox folder to display on the Home Screen. You'll know if a widget requires more information as a panel or window will appear after you drag the widget into place.

# Resize a widget

Some widgets are resizable, so you can make them as big or as small as you like. You'll be able to adjust the size of a widget immediately after adding it to the Home screen, but if you didn't get a chance at the time, simply **tap and hold** on an existing widget, then drag one of the **resizing dots** in or out.

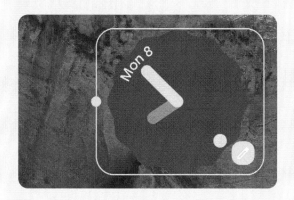

# Delete a widget

If you decide that you no longer need a widget on the Home screen, **tap and hold** on it, then when the grid appears, drag the widget upwards and on top of the **Remove** button.

# Connect to a Wi-Fi network

## Easily connect to home, office, or public Wi-Fi networks...

Connecting to a Wi-Fi network is one of those fundamental tasks that we all must do from time to time. Perhaps you're visiting a friend and would like to hook up to their internet connection, or you might be sat in a coffee shop that offers free Wi-Fi. Those who don't have unlimited data plans might also want to prevent a large bill from arriving at the end of the month. Whatever the reason, here's how you can connect to a new Wi-Fi network, disconnect from a network, and solve common problems...

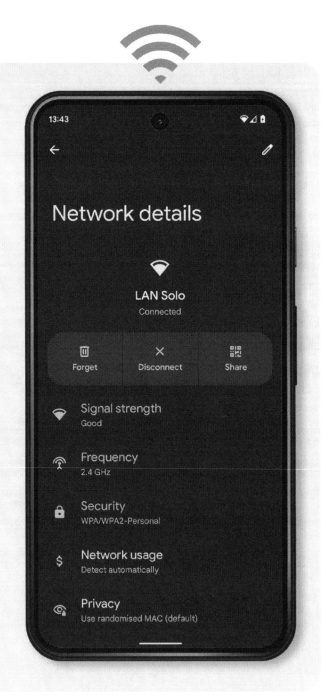

1. Swipe down from the top of the screen with two fingers. This will reveal the Quick Settings panel.

2. Tap the **Internet** button. You'll see it near the top of the screen.

3. If you live in a large house, then you should only see one Wi-Fi network. If you have neighbours nearby, then you might see multiple Wi-Fi networks available. That's because Wi-Fi signals can travel up to 50 meters, and even through walls. Think of it like a radio signal, and you'll get the idea.

4. Look for *your* Wi-Fi network then tap on it. If you don't which Wi-Fi network is yours, then you might need to ask whoever set it up for you. This might be a family member or friend, or it might be the network company.

5. After tapping on your Wi-Fi network, enter its password. If you don't know this, then try looking on the back of the Wi-Fi router. Usually a sticker can be found which contains the Wi-Fi password. You can also try asking whoever set up the Wi-Fi connection.

6. Tap the **Connect** button. If you've entered the password successfully your phone will automatically join the network.

# How to disconnect from a Wi-Fi signal

Sometimes you might need to disconnect from a Wi-Fi signal. Maybe you accidentally connected to it, or maybe you're in a hotel and don't want to pay for any further Wi-Fi access. To tell your phone to forget about a Wi-Fi network:

1. Swipe down from the top of the screen with two fingers. This will reveal the Quick Settings panel.

2. Tap the **Internet** button. You'll see it near the top of the screen.

3. Tap on the Wi-Fi network you wish to forget.

4. Tap **Disconnect**. If you don't want your phone to ever connect to the Wi-Fi network again, tap **Forget**.

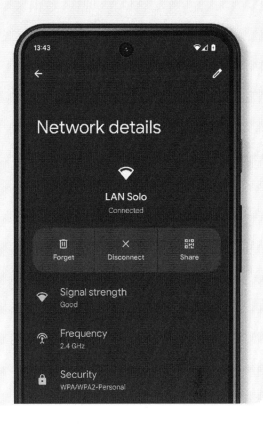

# What to do when the Wi-Fi stops working

If you're using the internet and it stops working, then you can usually remedy the problem by turning the router on and off again. To do this:

1. Look for the router. It's a small box connected to the phone line, and it likely looks like the image to the left. Often it has green blinking lights on one side. These lights indicate if the internet is working.

2. Restart the router. You can do this by pressing its power button, or by turning off the power at the wall, then back on again.

3. Wait for the router to turn back on. This can take up to two minutes, so be patient.

4. With a little luck, the internet will be working on your phone again.

# Add an email account

## Learn how to add your email account, and calendar events...

As you use your Android phone to explore the internet, you'll soon realise how important an email account is. It's basically a virtual postbox, letting you send and receive messages and register for services on the web. On this page, you'll learn the basics of adding an email account. Most of it happens automatically, and once you've added an account, you'll be able to start emailing friends and family, check your calendar for events, plus much more.

## Add your Google account

1. Start by opening the **Settings** app, then tap **Passwords & accounts**.

2. Tap on **Add Account**, then tap **Google**.

3. Sign in to your Google account by entering your email address and password. If you have two-factor authentication enabled, then follow the instructions to approve your device using a code or another device.

4. Your phone will verify your mail account details. Once the process has completed, you can choose whether you wish to sync mail, contacts, calendar events, notes, and more using the toggle buttons.

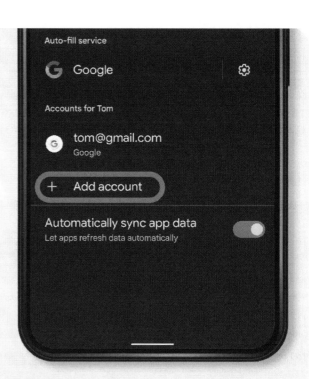

## Decide what to sync

After adding your Google account, you can sync a number of things with your phone, including contact numbers, documents, calendar events, notes, and purchases made via Google Play. To change what is synced and what isn't:

1. Go to **Settings** > **Passwords & accounts**, then tap on your **email address**.

2. Tap on **Account sync.**

3. Use the toggle switches to decide what to sync, and what not to sync.

# Add a custom email account

If you have a custom email account – perhaps with Outlook, Yahoo, or associated with work - then it's possible to enter its details and access your emails through the Mail app. Adding an account isn't as easy as simply entering a username and password; you'll also need the server details and choose whether to use IMAP or POP3 (explained shortly).

 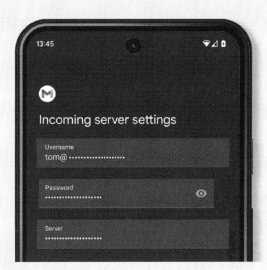

1. Start by opening the **Settings** app, then tap **Passwords & accounts**.

2. Tap on **Add Account**, then choose either **Personal (IMAP)** or **Personal (POP3)**. IMAP accounts store emails on a server, enabling you to check your email from multiple sources, i.e. your phone and a PC. A POP account stores emails only on your Android phone, meaning the account can only be accessed from that device.

3. In the Username field, enter the email address you would like to use. Next, enter the password used to access your account.

4. Tap **NEXT,** and your device will attempt to verify the account. If it cannot find the correct details, then enter either the IMAP or POP address into the **Server** field. You might need to ask your email provider for these details. Similarly, you might need the outgoing server address.

5. If everything is correct, then you'll be ready to send and receive emails via the Gmail app. You will also be able to sync contacts, calendar events and more (see back a page for more on this).

# Remove an account

If you no longer want to use an email or Google account with your Android phone, then:

1. Open the **Settings** app, then tap **Passwords & accounts**.

2. Tap on your **email address**, then tap **Remove account**. In the pop-up window, confirm your decision by tapping **Remove account**.

# Connect to Bluetooth devices

## Discover how to pair headphones and other Bluetooth devices...

The speakers in your phone do a pretty good job at playing music and audio, but by connecting a set of Bluetooth headphones, you can enjoy audio at a volume level that won't interrupt anyone else. It's not just headphones that you can connect, because Android supports a massive number of Bluetooth devices, including gaming controllers, microphones, and even fitness equipment such as treadmills.

## Connect a Bluetooth device

1. Open the **Settings** app, then tap **Connected Devices**.

2. Tap **+ Pair new device**.

3. Turn on the Bluetooth device you would like to connect to and make it discoverable. If you're not sure how to do that, read the device's instruction manual.

4. The Bluetooth device will appear in the Available devices panel. Tap on it to connect. If the device is a computer or a vehicle, then you may need to enter a pairing code.

5. The device will connect and appear in the Previously connected devices panel.

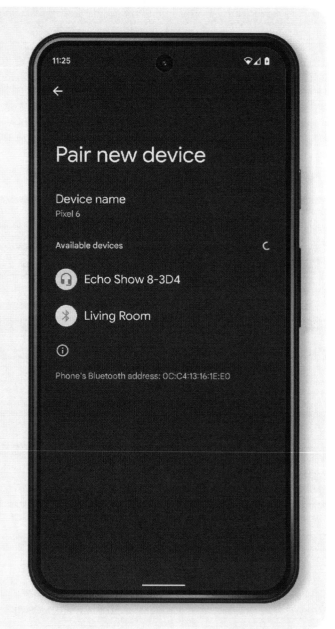

# Explore Bluetooth options

After a Bluetooth device has been paired, you can often customise it via the Connected devices Settings panel. For example, if you connect a pair of noise cancelling headphones, then it's possible to toggle noise cancellation, toggle media audio, share contacts (useful for making calls) and even which ear acts as a microphone. To find these settings:

1. Open the **Settings** app, then tap **Connected Devices**.

2. Under **Previously connected devices**, tap on the Bluetooth device, then make a choice.

# Swap between devices

If you're listening to music or talking to someone on the phone, and you want to swap from the speaker to your headphones, then:

1. Make sure the Bluetooth device is turned on and connected.

2. Swipe down from the top of the screen to access Quick Settings.

3. Look for the **playback** button. It's usually towards the top of the screen (see *fig. 1*).

4. Tap on **Phone speaker** (see *fig. 1*).

5. Use the panel at the bottom of the screen to select your Bluetooth device (see *fig. 2*).

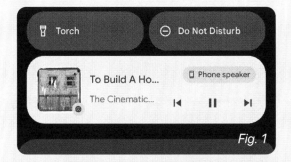

Fig. 1

Fig. 2

# Remove a Bluetooth device

If you no longer need to use a Bluetooth device, or you want to let someone else connect to it, then here's how to tell your Android phone to disconnect from it:

1. Open the **Settings** app, then tap **Connected Devices**.

2. Under **Previously connected devices**, tap on the Bluetooth device, then tap **Forget**.

# Access Quick Settings

## Discover how to quickly toggle controls...

Tucked above the screen are a helpful set of buttons for toggling settings and activating features. They include a slider for controlling the screen brightness, a button for enabling Wi-Fi, shortcuts to toggle Aeroplane Mode, set an alarm and more. To access these shortcuts at any time **swipe down from the top of the screen with two fingers**.

To close the Quick Settings panel, swipe upwards from the bottom of the screen, or tap the **Home** button if there's one on your device.

1. This is the brightness slider. It enables you to adjust the brightness of the screen by sliding it left or right.

2. Tap **Internet** to join a new Wi-Fi network, toggle Wi-Fi on or off, or disable your wireless signal.

3. Tap **Bluetooth** to toggle Bluetooth on or off. This can be helpful if you're having wireless connectivity issues, but it doesn't dramatically affect battery life, so it's best to leave it on.

4. If your Android phone has a camera flash on the back, then you can tap **Torch** to activate the flash and use it to find things in the dark.

5. If you don't want to be distracted by notifications, then tap **Do Not Disturb**.

6. Tap **Alarm** to quickly set an alarm for later in the day. From the same panel, you can also set a timer, stopwatch, or adjust Bedtime settings.

7. If you're boarding an aeroplane, then tap **Aeroplane mode** to disable your phone's wireless signal.

8. If you have any smart devices connected to your phone, such as smart lights, sockets, and locks, then tap this button to quickly control them.

9. Tap **GPay** to add a debit or credit card to your Google account. This will let you quickly buy things via a contactless reader without having to reach for your card each time.

10. Tap the **pencil** icon to edit the Quick Settings panel (see across the page for more).

11. Tap the **Power** button to restart or turn off your phone.

12. Tap **Settings** to open the Settings app.

# Find additional Quick Settings shortcuts

While the default controls in the Quick Settings panel are helpful for quickly adjusting brightness or toggling wireless features, there are a vast number of other toggle switches and shortcuts available. To find them, tap the **pencil** icon at the bottom of the Quick Settings panel.

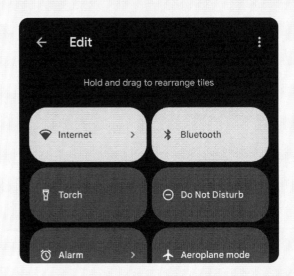

# Rearrange Quick Settings

After tapping the **pencil** button, you'll see a large number of Quick Setting shortcuts appear. So many, in fact, that they will run off the bottom of the screen. By default, only the top eight shortcuts will appear on the Quick Settings panel (you need to swipe them to the left to see more).

By rearranging the order of the shortcuts, you can decide what appears first. To do this, **tap and hold** on a Quick Settings shortcut, and then **drag it upwards** towards the top of the screen.

# Add Quick Settings

There are a number of additional Quick Setting shortcuts that you can add, including the ability to record the screen, toggle a Hotspot, and invert the screen's colours.

To add these, open the Quick Settings panel, tap the **pencil** button, then scroll down. Next, **tap and hold** on a Quick Setting shortcut, then **drag it upwards** towards the top of the screen. Let go when it's at the top, and it will then appear every time you open the Quick Settings panel.

Similarly, you can remove a shortcut from the Quick Settings by tapping the **pencil** button, then dragging the shortcut downwards towards the bottom of the screen.

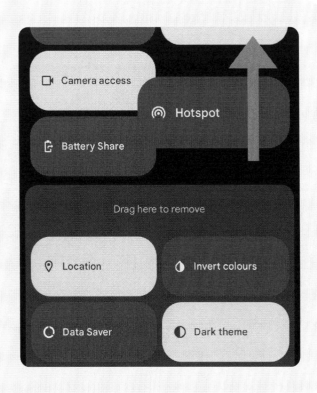

# Check your notifications

## Learn how to configure and manage alerts...

However you use your phone, you're going to receive notifications on a regular basis. Notifications usually appear when you have a new message, or if an app wants to get your attention. If your phone is locked, then the notification will appear as a bubble on the Lock screen. If you're using your device when the notification arrives, then it will appear as a floating panel at the top of the screen. If an app wants to get your attention, then you might see a red dot above its icon on the Home screen.

If there's one annoying aspect about receiving notifications on an Android phone, it's that you can't simply ignore them. Try to do that, and they'll only end up in the Notification Drawer, forever awaiting an action from yourself. Try and ignore that little red dot above an app icon, and it'll never go away. Thankfully, you can customise, hide, and even disable notifications from individual apps...

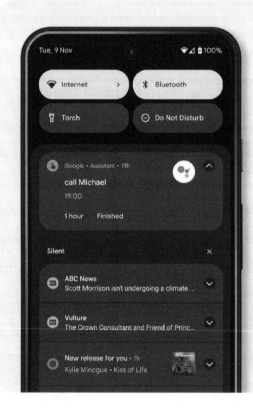

## Check the Notification Drawer

You can check for notifications at any time by swiping down from the top of the screen with one finger. Any notifications will appear below the four controls at the top of the screen.

**Note:** If you don't see any notifications, then you might have Do Not Disturb enabled. If so, tap the Do Not Disturb button to disable it, and any notifications that are waiting for you will appear.

## Clear a notification

To dismiss a notification, swipe across it from right to left. You'll see it dissapear, and never return.

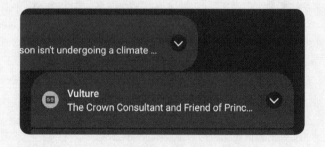

# Clear all of your notifications

If you want to clear away every single notification at once, scroll down to the bottom of them, then tap **Clear all**.

## See fewer notifications

If you don't want to continue recieving notifications from a particular app or service, then tap the small **arrow** on its right, and then tap **Fewer like this**.

# Turn off sounds for a notification

If you don't want to be pinged everytime there's a notification from an app or service, then **tap and hold** on the notification, then choose **Silent**.

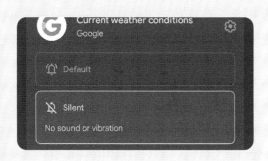

## Turn off notifications for a specific app

If you would like to ask an app to stop sending notifications, then here's how it works:

1. Open the **Settings** app, tap **Notifications**, then tap **App settings**.

2. To prevent ap app from sending notifications, toggle its switch **off**.

*Turn over for more on notifications...*

# Adjust specific notification settings for an app

Apps might send you notifications for a large number of reasons. You might have a new message, a breaking news story, or realtime map directions. If you're being distracted by unnessecary notifications from a specific app, then you can customise exactly what notifications you wish to recieve, and which you don't:

1. Open the **Settings** app, tap **Notifications**, then tap **App settings**.

2. Choose an app from the list. You will then see all the notification types that it will send. Here, for example, we can see that the Google News app will send you alerts for breaking news, daily top stories, featured content, plus much more.

3. To prevent notifications from a specific part or service of an app, simply toggle the relevant switch on or off.

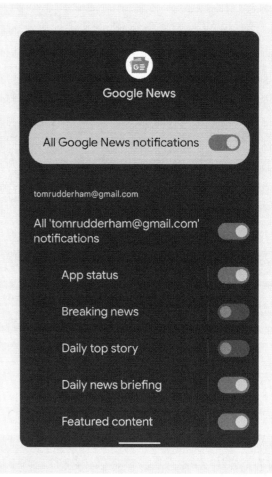

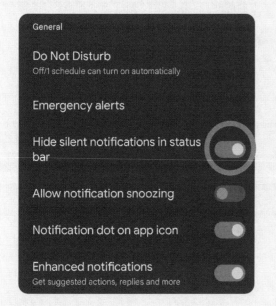

# Hide notifications from the status bar

The status bar runs along the top of your phone's screen. It shows the time, Wi-Fi strength, signal strength, and battery life. It also shows small notification icons, helping to alert you to new notifications. If you don't want to clutter the status bar with notification icons, then:

1. Open the **Settings** app, then tap **Notifications**.

2. Scroll down the screen, then toggle **Hide silent notifications in status bar** off. You will then see any icons in the status bar dissapear.

# Hide notification dots on app icons

If apps want to notify you about a new message, alert, or notification, then they will show a small dot on the upper-right side of the apps icon. To disable this feature:

1. Open the **Settings** app, then tap **Notifications**.

2. Scroll down the screen, then toggle **Notification dot on app icon** off.

# Disable enhanced notifications

Enhanced notifications can access personal information such as contact names and messages; then show suggested actions and replies that you can follow.

If you'd rather not let Android access this type of information, then go to **Settings** > **Notifications**, scroll all the way down and toggle off **Enhanced notifications**.

# Hide notifications on the Lock screen

By default, your phone will show notifications on the Lock screen, even conversations from friends and family. If you don't want anyone to see your messages, emails, and other notifications on the Lock screen, then:

1. Open the **Settings** app, then tap **Notifications**.

2. Tap on **Notifications on lock screen**.

3. Make a choice using the three options. You can show or hide conversions, or hide all notifications on the Lock screen.

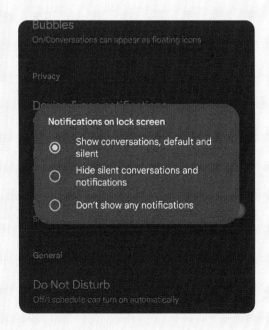

# Talk to Google Assistant

## Take command of your very own assistant...

Imagine Google Assistant as your very own personal assistant. He (or she depending on your country of origin) can make calls for you, dictate emails and messages, make a restaurant reservation, remind you to do things, tell you about movies, make jokes, and much more.

Google Assistant isn't perfect, however. It can't remember interactions from the past, it relies on hearing your voice in a clear manner, and it needs a connection to the internet to work. If you're aware of these limitations and don't mind the odd false request, then Google Assistant can save time and even be a little fun to use.

### Activate Google Assistant

To enable Google Assistant just hold down on the **Power** button. You can also say, "*Hey Google*" out-loud. You can now begin issuing commands.

### Speak to Google Assistant

Say out loud, "*What's the weather like today?*" Google Assistant will automatically look for a weather report then tell you what it's going to be like. It's that simple to use. When you're finished with Google Assistant, press the **Power** button to return to where you were before, or tap on the screen above it.

### Dictate text

If you'd like Google Assistant to dictate a message or an email, say something like, "*Tell Noah I'll be late*". Google Assistant will automatically create a new message or email to the recipient that says 'I'll be late home tonight'.

# Things you can ask Google Assistant...

"Remind me to call Michael at 7."

"Play something by Monsters and Men."

"Send a message to Dave."

"Set up a meeting with Sarah at 9."

"Email Chris to say I'm running late."

"Show me movies directed by Steven Spielberg."

"How do I get to Tom's?"

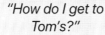

"What is the Microsoft stock price?"

"What are your best chat-up lines?"

"Do I look fat in this?"

"What's 15 plus 26 plus 12 plus 4?"

"Roll the dice." or "Flip a coin."

"Schedule a haircut on Tuesday at 1 p.m."

# Type on the keyboard

## The basics of the Android keyboard explained...

The software keyboard built into your Android phone is amazing in several ways. It guesses what word you're trying to write, then automatically finishes it for you. It rotates with the screen to make typing easier. You can hold down a key to see more options, plus much more. If you're new to typing on a glass screen then give it some time. The first few days might be frustrating as you work out how best to hold your phone. Personally, I like to hold my phone using both hands, and use my thumbs to type each key. Once you're comfortable typing, here are some tips for making the most out of your phone's keyboard...

## Make the keyboard bigger

To make the keyboard as big as possible, turn your phone on its side. This will ensure the keys are as large as possible, making it easier for you to tap on each one. Keep in mind that not every app will support a keyboard in the horizontal orientation, so some trial and error might be required.

## How to use the shift key

Notice the upward-facing arrow on the left side of the keyboard. This is the shift key. It lets you type capital letters, or even write entire sentences in capital letters.

Tap on the shift key once and the next character you type will be in capitals. Double-tap the shift key and everything you type will now be in capitals. You can also hold it down to type in capitals, then let go to return to lower case letters.

## Enter numbers and symbols

Notice the button in the left corner that says **?123**. By tapping this you can access keys for entering numbers, symbols, and even currencies. You can access further characters by tapping the button that says **=\<**, or return to the normal keyboard with **ABC**.

# Dictate text, rather than type it

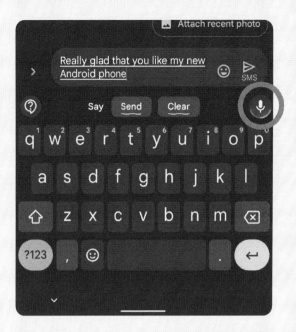

You can ask your phone to listen to your voice and turn it into text. It works surprisingly well, and if done right can save a lot of time.

To dictate text, look for the **microphone** button just above the keyboard. Tap on it and your phone will begin listening to you. Speak out loud, and watch as your phone enters text within the Text Message field. If you need to enter a comma, simply say *"comma"*. Similarly, if you need to enter a full stop, question mark, or exclamation mark, just say it out loud. When you've finished talking, tap the **microphone** button again. If you're composing a text message, then you can also say *"send"*.

# Send an emoji

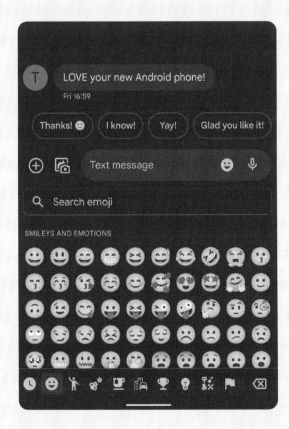

Think of emoji as a second language. One made primarily of pictures, rather than words. You can use them to inject some humour into a sentence, such as in this example:

### I absolutely 🤍 ☕ and 🍰

If you haven't already guessed, the above sentence says *"I absolutely love coffee and cake"*.

To send an emoji, tap the **smiley-faced** button in the Text Message field, just above the keyboard. The emoji keyboard will then appear, containing smiley faces, animals, symbols, and even flags. You can swipe through them to explore each category, or search for a particular emoji by typing something into the search field.

To add an emoji to your message, simply tap on it. If you need to return to the regular keyboard, then tap the **smiley-faced** button above the emoji panel.

# Type like a pro

## Become a master at typing with the Android keyboard...

Now that you're comfortable typing with the Android's keyboard, it's time to take a look at some of its more intelligent and advanced features. You might not know from looking at it, but the Android keyboard is capable of guessing what you're trying to type. It can even let you write words by swiping from one key to another.

## Create shortcuts

By creating your own dicationary shortcuts, you can type "*omw*" and your phone will automatically write "*On my way!*" To create your own shortcuts, go to **Settings > System > Languages and input > Personal dictionary.** On the following tap the **plus (+)** button to create your own phrase and shortcut.

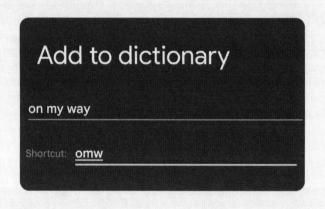

## Use predictive text

Predictive Text attempts to guess the next word you want to type and then offers it as a one-tap option above the keyboard.

To see predictive text in action, open the keyboard then start to type. As you enter each letter, a series of words will appear above the keyboard that guesses what you're trying to say. What makes predictive text really clever is that it learns who you're typing too and changes responses in relation to that person. So if you're talking to a close friend, predicted words will be relaxed and fun, but if it's your boss you'll see more formal and serious words appear.

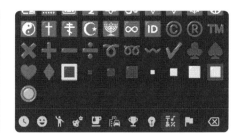

### Easily move the text cursor

If you'd like to quickly move the text cursor to another word or letter, **tap and hold** on the text you're writing, then drag the small green handle to a new location.

### Accents and extra keys

To add accents, extra letters and punctuation, **tap and hold** on a key. You'll see extra options and letters appear above your finger. To select one, simply drag your finger to it then let go.

### Add a trademark symbol

To find the trademark, copyright and registered symbols, open the **Emoji** keyboard then tap the character button that's second from the right. Swipe through the emojis a few times and eventually you'll see the trademark, copyright and registered symbols.

# Use swipe to type

If you'd rather write words by swiping from one letter to another, then you can do just this using the keyboard on your Android. Here's how it works:

1. Instead of tapping each key, place your finger on the first letter in a word, then swipe it to the next letter.

2. Keep on swiping from letter to letter until you've completed the word, then lift your finger.

3. There's no need to tap the spacebar, just start swiping the next word, and your phone will automatically enter a space.

With practice, you might find swiping to type even quicker than tapping each key, but keep in mind that you might make a few mistakes when you first try swiping. Like typing with two thumbs, swiping to type is a skill which takes time to master.

# How to copy and paste

## Discover how to copy something then paste it somewhere else...

Copying and pasting is a great way to move text or content from one app to another. For example, you could copy your address from Contacts and paste it into Chrome. Here's how it works:

### 1 Copy something

Find a source of text on your phone, perhaps your phone number in Contacts. **Tap and hold** your finger on the number, let go when the magnifying glass appears, then choose **Copy to clipboard** from the pop-up button.

### 2 Paste something

Next, close Contacts and open the Keep Notes app. Create a new note by tapping the **plus** icon, then **tap and hold** on the empty note and choose **Paste**. Your phone number will appear in the new note.

## A few more tips to help you select text:

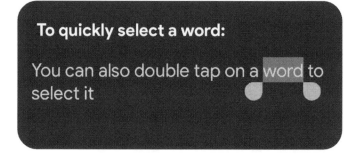

**To quickly select a block of text:**

Quickly select a block of text by dragging your finger across it

**To quickly select a word:**

You can also double tap on a word to select it

# How to share something

## Learn how to share something with other people or perform actions...

There's a lot you can do with a photo on your phone. You can edit it (which we cover in the Camera & Photos chapter), share it with friends, order it as a photo, and print it. The same goes for other things on your phone, like notes, reminders, and web pages. You can share all of these things (and more) by using the Share button. It's usually tucked away at the bottom of the screen and it looks like this:

## Share something with friends and family

When you tap the Share button, you'll see contact suggestions near the top of the panel. These are based on your recent activity with friends and family, so you might see a shortcut to email something, or attach it to a message.

## App shortcuts

Below the contact suggestions panel are a series of app shortcuts. If you decide to share a photo, you might see shortcuts for sending it within a message, posting it on Facebook, or attaching it within a note.

# Passwords

## Look up or manage your saved passwords...

Whenever you log into a website and enter a username, email address, or a password, your phone will ask if you would like to save these details on the device. If you agree, the next time you go back to the website and try to log in, your device will offer to automatically enter those details. It's a great time-saving feature, and it also means you don't have to remember every single password you've ever entered.

Sometimes you might need to take a look at these passwords and login details. Perhaps you're using someone else's computer and can't remember your password, or maybe you've accidentally saved multiple login details for a site and want to tidy them up. Here's how you can access every password and account saved on your Android phone in a few steps...

## View and edit your passwords

1. Open the **Chrome** app. Tap the **options** button (⋮) to the right of the address bar.

2. Tap **Settings**, then choose **Passwords**.

3. You can search for a website, username, email address, or password, by using the search field at the top of the screen.

4. Tap on a website to view the saved username and password. To edit any of these details, simply tap on them, make a change, then tap **Done**.

5. To delete a set of details, select it from the list, tap the **trash** button, then tap **Delete password**.

## Check your passwords for risk

You can ask your phone to look through all of your passwords and check for any that have been leaked onto the internet in data breaches. To do this go to the Passwords panel (see steps 1-3 above), then tap **Check passwords**. Any that are high risk will be flagged. You'll also see a button for changing the password on the appropriate website.

# Reset your Google password

If you have forgotten the password for your Google account, don't worry, as there are a couple of things you can try. The first is to change your password using your phone. To do this:

**1** Open the **Settings** app, then tap on your **profile photo** at the top of the screen.

**2** Tap **Manage your Google account**.

**3** Tap **Security**. If you can't see it, try sliding the links at the top of the screen towards the left.

**4** Under "Signing in to Google," tap **Password**.

**5** You might be asked to enter your account password. If you've forgotten it, tap **Forgot password?** and follow the instructions to reset your password. Otherwise, enter your new password then tap **Change password**.

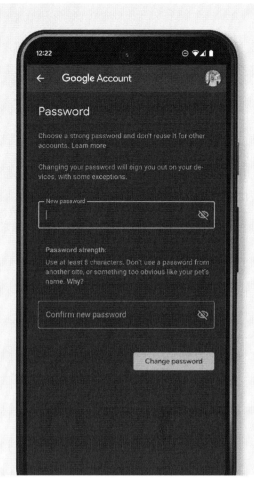

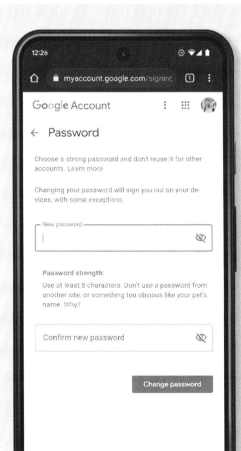

# Reset your Google password on the internet

If the above steps didn't work, then you can try resetting your password on the Google website. To do this:

**1** Use a web browser (such as Chrome) and go to **myaccount.google.com**

**2** If you're not already logged in, tap **Go to Google Account**. If you've forgotten your details, click **Forgot email / password?**

**3** Once logged in, tap **Security**. If you can't see it, try sliding the links at the top of the screen towards the left.

**4** Under "Signing in to Google," tap **Password**. If you're asked to log in again, enter your password. On the following screen, enter your new password then tap **Change password**.

# An overview of apps

## What are apps, and how to find them...

Your Android phone is pretty clever straight out of the box. It can take calls, check the news, let you send messages, and so much more. Each of these services is provided by a unique app. Think of an app as a shortcut to something, so if you want to look at your photos, then you open the Photos app. Similarly, if you want to look through your phone book contacts, then you open the Contacts app.

There are a lot of apps on your phone, and they might differ depending on the phone's manufacturer, but here are the apps you can expect to find on every Android device:

**Calculator**
You guessed it, this app lets you perform calculations.

**Calendar**
Add and view appointments, birthdays, and other reminders.

**Camera**
Take photos and videos with your phone.

**Chrome**
Browse and navigate the internet.

**Contacts**
Your very own phone book, where you can create and edit contacts.

**Docs**
Create letters and documents on your phone.

**Drive**
Access all of the files, folders, and downloads saved in your Google account.

**Duo**
Make free video calls to friends and family who also have an Android and Google account.

**Files**
See all of the downloads, images, and files saved on your device.

**Gmail**
Read and compose emails.

**Google**
A shortcut to Google, right on your phone.

**Google Pay**
Add a debit or credit card to your phone, then use it at contactless readers to make payments.

**Keep Notes**
A pocket notebook, where you can enter text, make lists, and even add tables.

**Maps**
View aerial or classic maps of the entire world. You can also get directions and information for businesses and places.

**Messages**
Send instant messages to friends and family.

**News**
Read the latest news stories from various sources within your country.

**Phone**
Make phone calls to friends and loved ones.

**Photos**
View all of the photos and videos taken on your device. You can also share them, view them in albums, and view slideshows.

**Play Store**
Browse and install apps for your phone. You'll also find movies, TV shows, and books to read.

**Settings**
Access all the settings for your phone, set restrictions, and customise notifications.

# See all the apps on your phone

As we explored on page **21**, there are a lot of apps pre-installed on your phone. You can find them in the App Drawer. To access it, swipe upwards on the Home Screen, and you'll see a grid of apps appear with a search box above. Feel free to browse through the apps on your phone, or if there's a specific app you're looking for, use the search box.

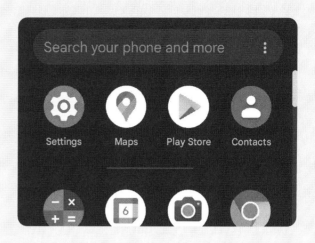

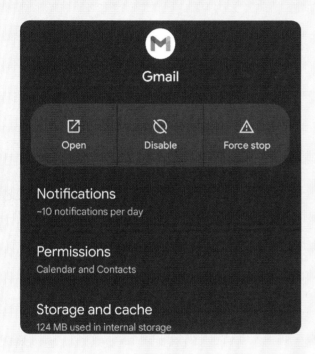

# View information about an app

From the App Drawer screen, **tap and hold** on an app and then tap the **App info** button. Sometimes you might see an **(i)** icon instead. On the following screen, you'll see the following pieces of information:

* How many notifications the app has sent per day.
* A shortcut to the permissions an app has.
* How much storage the app is using on your phone.
* How much data the app has used.
* How long you've spent using the app.
* How much battery life the app has used during the last 24 hours.
* Whether the app is the default choice (for example, Gmail can be the default app for checking emails).

# Icons used throughout Android

As you start to use apps on your phone, you might start to recognise icons that are used throughout apps and the wider interface. Here's an overview of the most common icons you can expect to see:

**Options**. Displays a list of actions you can perform.

**Add**. Enables you to create another item.

**Close**. Clears something away, such as text in an input field, or an item in a list.

**Share**. This action will let you share something, such as a photo or document, to other people.

**Settings**. Enables you to adjust the preferences for an app.

**Menu**. Also known as a "hamburger menu", this will display a meu of content.

**Search**. Enables you to find something within an app or on your phone.

**Refresh**. Enables you to reload a page. Helpful if a website has stopped loading content.

# Explore the Play Store

## Discover an unlimited number of apps for your phone...

Your Android phone might come with a large number of apps pre-installed; but if you want to do something specific, such as watch Netflix, make a Zoom video call, or play a video game, then you'll need to visit the Play Store, where there are millions more apps to discover.

Think of the Play Store as a shopping centre, but for apps and media. To find it, look for this icon:

Open the Play Store, and it's hard not to be overwhelmed by the sheer number of apps, games, movies, and books available. You'll initially see highlighted apps for the day. This is curated by a team within Google, and they usually handpick some of the most inventive and fun apps out there. Look at the bottom of the screen, and you'll see shortcuts to the latest games, apps, movies, TV shows, and books. If you already know what app you want to install, then use the search bar at the top of the screen to find it.

# How to install an app

To install an app, just tap the **INSTALL** button if it's a free app, or the **price** button if it's a paid app.

If you're logged into your Google account, then the app will automatically install. You can then find it by opening the App Drawer.

# Check out user reviews

If you're unsure about an app, then it's usually a good idea to see what everyone else is saying about it. To do this, go to the app in the Play Store, then scroll down. You'll then see an average rating for the app, alongside recent reviews by other people who have installed the app.

# How to review an app

Want to tell others about how great (or terrible) an app is? First, make sure you've already downloaded the app, then head over to its page in the Play Store. Next, scroll down to the user reviews section (as mentioned above), then tap one of the stars in the **Rate this app** section. One star represents a poor app, while five stars represent a perfect app. After tapping a star, you'll be able to describe your experience with the app and tag the app with keywords.

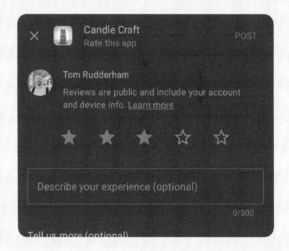

# Check out movies, TV shows, and books

It's not just apps that you'll find in the Play Store. Look at the bottom of the screen, and you'll see shortcuts for exploring the latest movies, TV shows, and books. Each section is broken down into genres, so it's easy to find precisely what you're looking for.

# Top social media apps

## Keep in touch with friends and family...

With large pin-sharp displays, Android phones are a great way to make video calls to friends and family. They're also helpful for sharing photos and writing heartfelt messages to loved ones. To get you started, here are a few social media apps used by millions around the world. You can find them by opening the Play Store then using the search feature:

 **Facebook**

The number one social media platform in the world, Facebook is a great way to keep in touch with friends and family. It also has its very own marketplace for finding local bargains.

 **Messenger**

You'll need a Facebook account to use Messenger, but once signed up, you can send messages to friends and family and even make free video calls.

 **Instagram**

Share photos and videos with others around the world. Where Instagram differs from other social media platforms is that it enables you to follow celebrities - not just your friends and family.

 **TikTok**

TikTok is focused entirely around short video clips, mostly themed around dance, lip-sync, comedy, and upcoming talent. With its focus on fast-paced entertainment, it's easily possible to lose an entire evening scrolling through silly video clips.

 **Pinterest**

For the creative type, Pinterest can provide a continuous source of inspiration. It enables you to share and discover recipes, home ideas, artwork, style inspiration, and more.

 **Twitter**

With a limit of just 280 characters, Twitter is focused entirely on efficient communication. It's used by presidents, businesses, celebrities, and regular folks alike, and stands alongside Facebook as one of the biggest social media networks on the planet.

 **LinkedIn**

Think of LinkedIn as a social media platform for careers. After creating a profile detailing your career and skills, you're able to search for jobs, and network with similar people.

 **Reddit**

One of the biggest, oldest, and most diverse communities on the web. While it has a homepage displaying the most popular news stories of the day, Reddit is actually compromised of endless "subreddits", each focused around a subject such as Star Wars, Art, Memes, and more.

 **WhatsApp**

Arguably the number one chat app in the world, used by hundreds of millions of people across all brands of smartphone devices. It also supports free audio and video calls. Chances are someone you know uses WhatsApp to communicate.

# Top productivity apps

## Edit a complex spreadsheet, set timed breaks, and more...

It might have a pocket-sized screen, but it's still possible to edit spreadsheets and create presentations on an Android phone. To get you started, here are a few apps focused around productivity and timekeeping...

### Microsoft Word

Yes, you can get Microsoft Word for Android phones, enabling you to create documents and letters on the go.

### Microsoft Powerpoint

Create beautiful presentations and slideshows, all on your Android phone using just your fingertips.

### Microsoft Excel

If you need to create spreadsheets on your phone, then Excel is the app of choice; and it works surprisingly well on a touchscreen.

### Microsoft Office

There are individual apps available (as we mentioned above), but this takes the basics from each and combines them into a single app. You can open and edit Office files, create PDFs, and access your personal cloud storage.

### Brain Focus

Let yourself focus better at work with this useful app that lets you set timed breaks, disable notifications, and block certain apps.

### Task Agenda

Task Agenda is a combination of a notepad, task manager and journal. If you're someone who attends a lot of meetings and makes important decisions throughout the day, then Task Agenda will help you track your tasks and thoughts.

### Grammarly

Grammarly is a professional text editor and spell checker, able to improve your writing and grammar in real-time. It will suggest alternative words, fix broken sentences, and generally help to improve anything you write.

### Site Audit Pro

A regular bestseller in the App Store, Site Audit Pro is focused around auditing and inspections, enabling businesses to easily perform audits, quotations, safety inspections and more.

# Top utility apps

## Check the weather, track your calorie intake and more...

The smartphone is truly the pocket-knife of the 21st century, with the ability to become nearly any tool you need. Whether you're looking for an accurate weather forecast, want to know which stars and planets are overhead, or want to monitor your calorie intake, these are the best apps available...

 **Weather**

Live forecast updates are at your fingertips with The Weather Channel. Get the local weather forecast news delivered directly to your phone. Prepare with severe weather reports and live radar maps.

 **MyFitnessPal**

If you're serious about losing weight, then MyFitnessPal is the best app you can install. It enables you to build a daily diary of calorie intake by scanning the barcode on food and drink, track your weight over time, and set a daily calorie limit.

 **SkyView**

Simply point your phone at the night sky, and this app will tell you precisely what planets, stars, satellites and constellations are in front of you. A free version (SkyView Lite) is also available if you want to try this app for free.

 **Airbnb**

Look for unique hotels, experiences, and places to stay around the world. You'll never struggle to find somewhere interesting, with locations suitable for holidays and business trips alike.

 **KAYAK Flights**

Find cheap flights or hotels around the world with this travel-based app. What makes it stand out from similar apps is the ability to chain multiple flights together, but the ability to also book hotels and explore destinations really add to the experience.

 **Microsoft Bing**

If you're looking for an alternative to Google, then Bing does a great job at providing search results, maps, and trending stores. You can also personalise the apps home screen with stunning wallpaper images from around the world.

 **Tripadvisor**

With more than 700 million reviews from travellers around the world, the Tripadvisor app is a great way to find and compare hotels, restaurants and attractions.

 **Shazam**

If there's a song playing in the background that you don't recognise, Shazam will identify it for you, then let you know where it can be purchased or streamed.

 **Rightmove**

Whether you're looking to buy or rent a property, RightMove is the number one app of choice. Nearly every property on the market is listed here, and it's easy to filter search parameters based on price, location, and more.

# Top shopping and food apps

## Order takeaway food or shop for any item on earth...

If you're looking to shop, sell, find food or look for culinary inspiration, these Android apps are all you need.

 **Amazon**

With the most significant digital store in the world, and the ability to buy nearly anything with a single tap, the Amazon app is an essential download for your phone.

 **Wallmart**

Shop online to order fresh groceries, household essentials, and more for pickup or delivery from your local store, plus millions of items available with free shipping.

 **eBay**

The biggest auction site on the planet, eBay lets you bid, buy, or sell nearly anything you can imagine.

 **Etsy**

Think of Etsy as the worlds number one shop for handmade and one-of-a-kind items. Using the app, you can shop for items, chat directly with shop owners, and get notifications.

 **Deliveroo**

Feeling hungry? The Deliveroo app is the perfect way to discover takeaway food in your area, order and pay for it, then track it in realtime as the delivery driver brings it to your door.

 **Yelp**

Using the Yelp app, you can search for restaurants in your area, check out the opening hours, menu, and even book a table.

 **ChefsFeed**

If you're planning to stay in and cook for the night, ChefsFeed is a brilliant way to find inspiration. Using the app, you can take part in live interactive classes, discover recipes and ideas, or find the best restaurants and bars in your area.

 **Cocktail Flow**

Cocktail Flow features beautifully presented cocktail recipes with step by step guides and features you'll love whether you're a novice bartender or a professional mixologist.

 **Uber Eats**

If you didn't find the right dish on Deliveroo, then Uber Eats is a good backup choice. It covers most large cities, and is often priced competitive with its rivals.

# Use Chrome to browse the web

## Visit websites, organise tabs, customise your experience, and more...

The Chrome app is the very best way to browse the web on your Android phone. It's blazingly fast, rendering web pages in an instant. It can strip all the ads and junk out of a page to show you only the content you want to see, it automatically blocks pop-ups, and so much more.

You'll find the Chrome app already installed on your phone. To locate it, just tap on this icon:

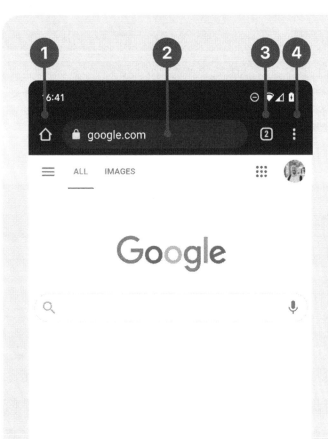

## The basics

**1** This is a shortcut to the **Chrome homescreen**. See across the page for more.

**2** This is the **search bar.** You can tap on it then search for websites, people, objects, and anything else that you can thing of.

**3** This is the **tabs** button. Tap this to see an overview of all the tabs open on your device (turn over for more on tabs).

**4** This is the **options** button. Tap it to see the following:
- App settings.
- Your browsing history.
- Downloaded files.
- Bookmarks.
- Share content.
- Translate a page.
- Add a shortcut to the Home screen.
- View the desktop version of a website.

## Visit a website

To visit a website, open **Chrome**, then tap on the **address field** at the top of the screen. Next, enter the website's address, then tap the blue **Go** button on the keyboard.

# Search the internet

The address bar in Chrome also acts as a search engine, so to search the web for any question or search term, just type your query into the address bar at the top of the screen.

# Visit Chrome's homepage

Tap the **Home** button in the upper-left corner, and you'll be taken to Chrome's homepage. From here, you can search google, see your most frequently visited websites, and see the latest news based on your browsing history.

# Use tabs to visit more than one website

Think of a tab as a single sheet of paper within a notebook. Using tabs, you can open multiple websites at once on your device. To see all the tabs on your phone, tap the **tabs** button in the upper right corner of the screen. It usually has a number within a square indicating the total number of tabs open on your phone.

# Explore your tabs

When you are in the tab view, you can see an overview of all the tabs open on your phone.

To open a new tab view, press the **plus (+)** button in the upper-left corner.

To close a tab, press the small **X** button in it's top-right corner.

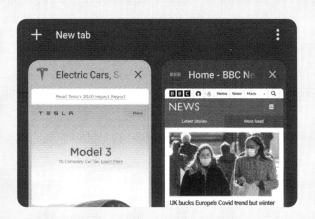

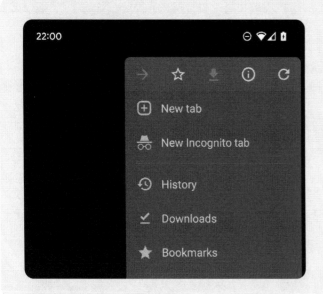

# Browse Incognito

Chrome has a built-in privacy mode called Incognito. While browsing the web in this mode, your browsing history, passwords, and settings are not saved.

To start browsing in Incognito mode, tap the **options** button in the upper-right corner, then choose **New Incognito tab**. When you're ready to return to the usual browsing mode -- where everything is saved -- tap the **tabs** button in the upper-right corner, then tap the **numbered tabs** button.

# Add a bookmark

If you visit a website regularly then it's a good idea to bookmark it. This lets you easily re-visit the website by tapping the **options** button in the upper-right corner, then **Bookmarks**.

To add a new bookmark, tap the **options** button in the upper-right corner of the screen, then tap the **star** button.

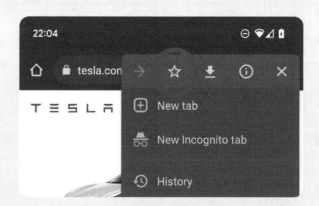

# View and manage your bookmarks

To quickly visit your bookmarks, tap the **options** button in the upper-right corner, then tap **Bookmarks**.

To remove a Bookmark, tap the **options** button to its right, then choose **Delete**.

To edit the details of a bookmark, such as its URL and name, tap the **options** button to its right, then choose **Edit**.

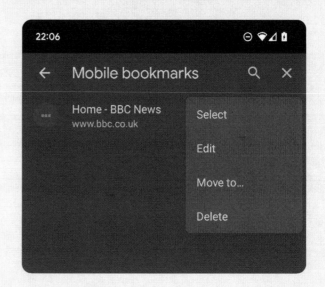

# Look something up

If you want to find out more about a word, phrase, or product, then **tap and hold** on its text, then tap on the small **information bar** that appears at the bottom of the screen. You'll then see Google search results for the text you selected.

# Find out more about an image or product

If you see a photo of a product, object, landmark or animal, and want to find out more about it, then **tap and hold** on the image, then choose **Search image with Google Lens** in the pop-up panel. Your phone will then look for visual matches on the web, and offer a wealth of information.

# Share a website

Sometimes it's helpful to share a website with friends and family. Chrome offers a wealth of sharing options, including the ability to email web pages, send a website via the messages app, and much more.

To access these sharing abilities, tap the **options** icon in the upper-right corner of the screen (it looks like three dots stacked on top of each other), then choose **Share**. You'll see the share panel slide up the screen, with icons and shortcuts to each sharing ability. Tap on whichever is most suitable for your needs. In the example below, I have shared a website and selected the Messages app.

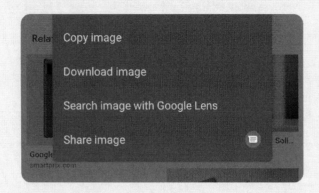

# Download a photo

The term "download" is often misused or misunderstood. What it means is to save something from the internet and then keep it on your phone. Let's say you come across a photo on the internet and want to save it to your device. To do this, **tap and hold** on the image, then in the pop-up panel, tap **Download Image**.

# Exploring your downloads

To access anything you've downloaded from the internet, open Chrome, tap the **options** button in the upper-right corner, then choose **Downloads**. You'll then see a grid-based layout of your recent downloads.

If you have been particularly busy downloading files, then you can use a search box to find something specific.

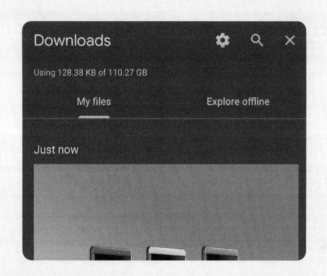

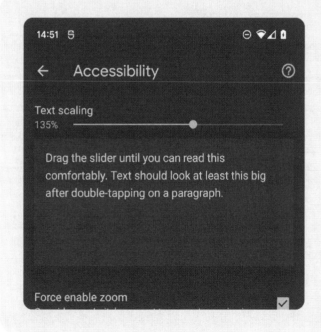

# Adjust text size

If you're struggling to read text on websites and articles, then Chrome has a helpful feature for increasing text size across every website you visit. Here's how it works:

**1** Open Chrome, then tap the **options** button in the upper-right corner.

**2** Tap **Settings,** then choose **Accessibility**.

**3** Use the Text scaling slider to adjust text size. The more you slide the control to the right, the larger text will appear. You can see a preview of how text will appear within websites below the slider.

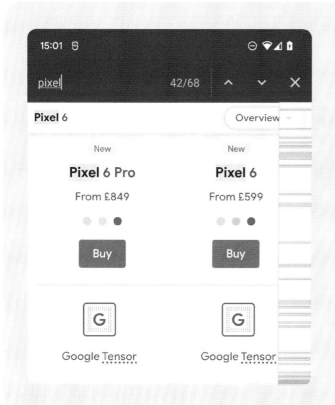

# Search a web page for text

If you're browsing a long web page or article, and want to find something specific, then tap the **options** button in the upper-right corner, then choose **Find in page**. Next, use the keyboard to type a word or phrase, then press the blue button on the bottom of the keyboard. You will then see any instances of the word or phrase highlighted in yellow.

Notice the yellow lines running down the right side of the screen. This isn't a graphical anomaly but rather a preview of where any highlighted words can be found. Try tapping on a yellow line, or run your finger up and down the panel, and you'll quickly skip through the page.

# Translate text

If you come across a website in another language, and want to read the content in English, then Chrome can translate more than 100 lanuages into English. You can even translate English pages into one of these other languages. To do this:

**1** While reading a webpage, tap the **options** button in the upper-right corner.

**2** Tap **Translate...**

**3** Chrome will attempt to automatically recognise the language on the page, then translate it to English.

**4** If you would like to translate the page to another language, then tap the **options** button in the translate panel at the very bottom of the screen, then tap **More languages**. You can then pick another language using the pop-up panel.

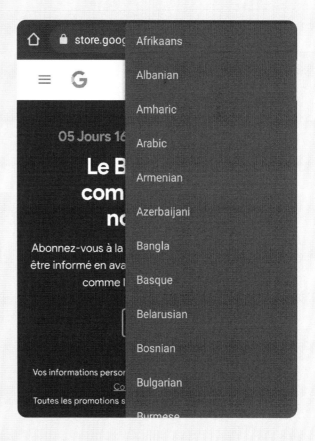

# Chat using Messages

## Send messages, photos, and even voice recordings...

If you want to send a text message, photo, video, or even a voice message, then the Messages app is the best way to do it. It's completely free if you're sending a message to someone else with an Android device), and if you want to text someone with an iPhone, then you'll only pay what your network provider charges.

To find the Messages app, look for the blue app icon with a speech bubble:

## The basics

**1** Tap the **arrow** to return to the main menu of the Messages app, where you can select other conversations

**2** If the person you're talking to also has an Android device, then tap this button to begin a video call with them.

**3** Start a phone call with the other person.

**4** Search your entire conversation with someone, for keywords, numbers, or phrases.

**5** Tap the **options** button to see details about the person (or people) in a conversation, archive the chat, or delete it from your phone.

**6** Tap the **plus (+)** button to search for an animated GIF image or share your location (helpful if you're meeting someone).

**7** Send a photo to the person/s in the conversation. You can either take a photo on the spot or send one from your phone's image library.

**8** Send an emoji to the other person.

**9** **Tap and hold** on this button to send an audio message to someone. This can be helpful if you have a lot to say, but not a lot of time to write.

# Send a message

Open the Messages app, then tap the **Start Chat** button in the lower-right corner of the screen.

In the **To**: field, type the phone number of someone you know. If you have already added them to the Contacts app, then you can also type their name.

Once you've entered someone's details, tap the **text entry** field just above the keyboard, then type a message. Once you're ready to send, tap the **blue arrow** button on the keyboard and the message will be sent to the recipient.

# Send a photo

If you would like to send a photo or video to someone, then tap the small grey **arrow** button to the left of the compose field, then tap the photo button which appears.

To send a photo on the spot, tap the white **shutter** button in the camera preview window. To send a photo that's already saved on your phone, tap the **Gallery** button and then make a choice.

# Send a voice message

Sometimes it's easier to send a voice message to someone, especially if you have a lot to say.

To do this, **tap and hold** the **voice message** button to the right of the compose field. As you hold down the button, say your voice message out loud. When you're finished, let go of the button. You can then preview the message and send it by tapping the **blue arrow**.

# Dictate a text message

If you struggle to type on the Android keyboard, then it's possible to dictate a text message out loud. Your phone will listen carefully and input what you say, and it's even possible to add grammar with simple commands.

To dictate a text message, tap the **microphone** button that sits above the "p" key. You'll hear a chime, and your phone will start listening to your voice. Say your message out loud, then when you're ready to send it, pause for a moment, and then say "send" out loud.

To help you dictate a message, here are some of the other voice commands you can use:

*"Stop".* Stop dictating and close the microphone.

*"Delete".* Deletes the last word.

*"Clear".* Removes the last sentence.

*"Clear all".* Deletes all text.

*"Lol emoji"* Inserts the laugh out load emoji.

*"Heart emoji".* Inserts the love emoji.

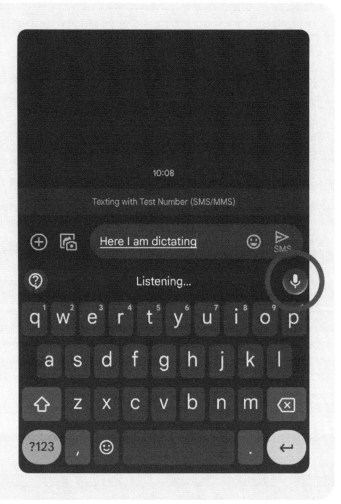

# Delete a chat

There are two ways to remove chat conversations from the Messages app. The simplest is to **swipe right-to-left** across the chat conversation from the home page of the Messages app. Alternatively, **tap and hold** on the conversation, then tap the **trash** button at the top of the screen (see below).

# Pin contacts

If you talk to someone regularly, then it's a good idea to pin them to the top of the Messages home page. To do this, **tap and hold** on their chat conversation, then tap the **pin** button at the top of the screen. To remove them at a later date, simply **tap and hold** on their conversation, then tap **Unpin**.

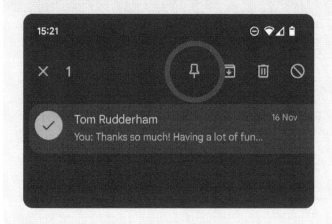

# Send an emoji

To send an emoji, tap the **Emoji** button on the keyboard while composing a message. It's at the bottom of the screen next to the microphone. You can drag the emoji panel upwards to see more of them, or tap the grey icons at the bottom of the screen to jump to an emoji category.

# Search for emoji

There are a bewildering amount of emojis to choose from, so it can often be a chore to find the perfect response. Thankfully a search bar above the emoji keyboard lets you look for a specific emoji. It will also suggest similar emojis that you might want to use.

# Find replacement words and check spelling

If you're struggling to think of the perfect word or phrase, then your Android phone can come up with some helpful suggestions. It can also check for spelling mistakes and alternative phrases:

1. Start by composing your message. It can be as short or as long as you'd like.

2. To find a replacement word, tap on it within the compose field, then tap a suggestion that appears below (see image to the right).

3. This works with spelling and grammer too. Try tapping on a word and if there's a fix or suggestion, then you'll see it above the keyboard.

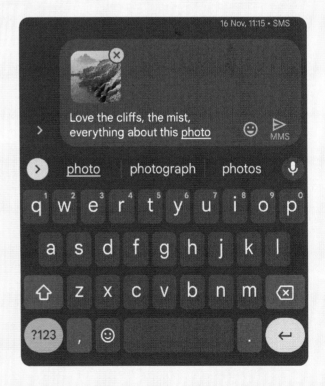

# Search a conversation

If you've been chatting to someone for a while, and you want to find something they said at an earlier date, then open the conversation then tap the **magnifying glass** icon at the top of the screen.

Next, search for a word or phrase, then tap the search query below, or the search button on the keyboard. You'll then see highlighted results for any successful search results.

# Toggle light or dark theme

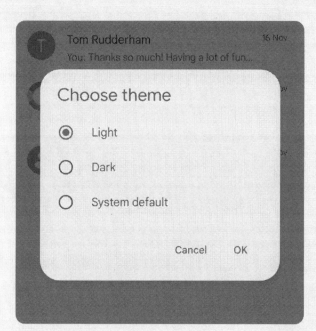

By default, the Messages app on Android has a dark appearance. If you'd rather see a brighter, lighter theme, then:

1. Go to the main overview screen where you can see all of your conversations.

2. Tap the **options** button on the right side of the search bar at the top of the screen.

3. Tap **Choose theme**.

4. Make a choice using the pop-up window, then tap **OK** to save your choice.

# Hide read receipts

Whenever you read a message from someone, they will see a small piece of text on their screen to let them know that you have read the message. If you'd prefer some privacy, then here's how to hide this feature:

1. Go to the main overview screen where you can see all of your conversations.

2. Tap the **options** button on the right side of the search bar at the top of the screen, then choose **Settings**.

3. Choose **Chat features**, then toggle **Send read receipts** off.

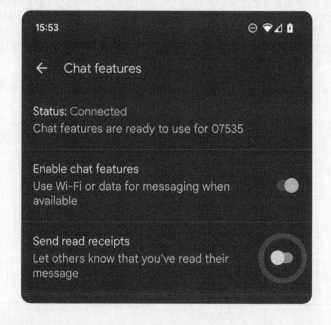

# Check for spam or blocked messages

Your Android phone will automatically block any obvious spam messages. This is a really helpful way to ensure you're not inundated with junk and spam, but occasionally a message you're waiting for might not come through due to a false positive.

To check whether a message you're expecting has been marked as spam:

**1** Go to the main overview screen where you can see all of your conversations.

**2** Tap **Spam and blocked**.

**3** Any marked messages will then appear. If there are no messages to be found, then it's likely the sender has either not sent the message, or it has gone to the wrong number.

# Get SMS delivery reports

If you would like to know when a message has been received by the recipient, then the Messages app can display the word "Delivered" below the message bubble. To enable this feature:

**1** Go to the main overview screen where you can see all of your conversations.

**2** Tap the **options** button on the right side of the search bar at the top of the screen, then choose **Settings**.

**3** Tap **Advanced**.

**4** Look for **Get SMS delivery reports**, then toggle the switch on to activate this feature.

# Quickly block someone

If you want to block a number and mark it as spam, then **tap and hold** on their chat conversation, then tap the **block** button at the top of the screen.

A pop-up window will then appear. Tap **OK** to confirm your choice. You can also report the number to Google and let them know it is sending spam. This will help Google to recognise future spam messages and prevent them from being sent to other people.

# Send an email

## Compose messages, organise your inbox, and more...

Alongside the Messages app, Gmail must come close to being on the most used apps on Android. That's because if you're serious about doing things on the web, like shopping or registering for services, then there's no way to avoid having an email address — it's a basic requirement for so many things.

Thankfully, the Gmail app is easy to use and gets straight to the point. It's designed with a clean interface that helps you focus on what's important: your emails, and it can even guess what you're trying to say.

To find the Gmail app, unlock your Android phone, then tap on this icon:

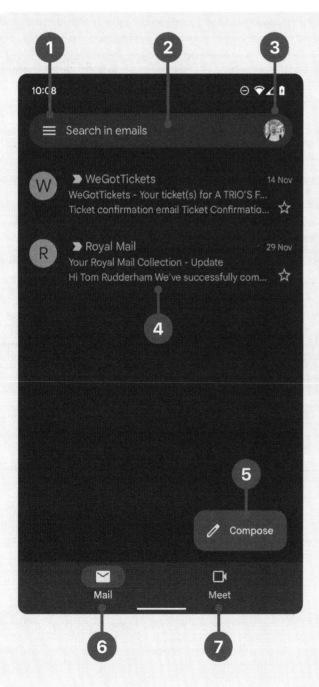

## The basics

**1** Tap the **menu** button to jump between folders, tags, snoozed emails, sent emails, drafts, your calendar, contacts, and settings.

**2** If you're looking for a specific contact, word, or subject, then use the **search bar** to quickly scan through your entire email account.

**3** Tap on your **profile photo** to manage your account, add another account, or manage accounts on your device.

**4** Tap on an email to open and read it. You can also **tap and hold** on an email to archive it, delete it, mark it as unread or favourite it.

**5** You might have guessed what this button does: it enables you to compose a brand new email. See across the page for more.

**6** This button acts as a shortcut to the main inbox for your email account (as seen in this photo).

**7** Tap **Meet** to start a video meeting with someone in your contacts book. To learn more about meetings, jump to page **81**.

# Send an email

When you're ready to send an email, tap the **Compose** button in the lower bottom right corner. You'll then see the compose window slide into view. Here's an overview of what each field does:

- **To**: In the To: field, type the email address of the person or organisation that you wish to email. Tap the small **downwards arrow** to access the following two fields:

- **Cc**: In this field, enter the email addresses of people that you want to include, but are not addressing directly.

- **Bcc**: Anyone in this field will receive your email, but won't see the other email addresses of anyone else included in the message.

- **Subject**: Type a short title to describe your email.

In the space below, type your email. When you're ready to send, tap the **arrow** in the top right corner.

# Format text

If you'd like to bold, italicise or underline a word or sentence, highlight the text by tapping on it, tap on the **Format** option in the pop-up window, then use the controls above the keyboard to bold, italicise, or underline text.

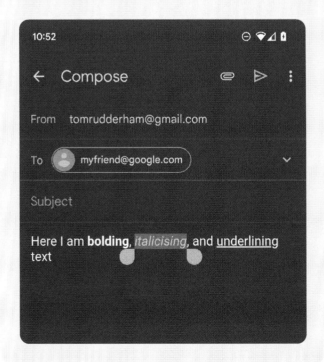

# Attach images

To attach an image within an email, tap where you want it to go, tap the **attachment** button at the top of the screen, then choose **Attach file**. On the following screen, select **Images**, then either choose a recent photo, or tap **Photos** to access your entire image library. Notice how you can also attach videos, audio, and documents with an email using the shortcuts at the top of the screen.

# Colour text

Adding colour to text is a good way to emphasise something. Using the Gmail app, you can add colour to text and even add a coloured background. To do this, highlight the text by tapping on it, then tap on the **Format** option in the pop-up window. You'll see a selection of controls appear above the keyboard. Tap the **underlined A** button to colour text, or tap the **paint bucket** to add colour behind text.

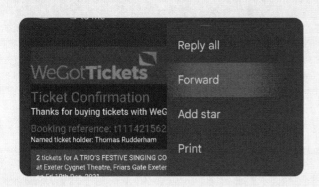

# Forward an email

To quickly forward an email to someone else, open the email, tap the **options** button on the right side of the screen, then choose **Forward**. A new window will then appear, enabling you to enter a contact's email address and tap **Send**.

# Star an email

If you receive an important email, or perhaps an email that you would like to save for the future, then open it and tap the **star** button near the top of the screen.

The email will then be saved to your Starred folder. To access this, return to the main panel of Gmail where your inbox can be seen, tap the **menu** button in the top left corner, then choose **Starred**.

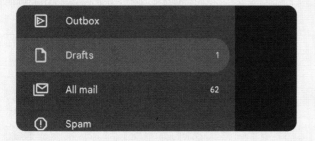

# Save a draft email

If you're not ready to send it yet, tap the **back** arrow in the top left corner and your email will be saved to the Drafts folder. To access your draft messages, tap the **menu** button from the inbox, then choose **Drafts**.

# Refresh the inbox

If you're waiting for an important email and it hasn't arrived yet, then you can force Gmail to check for new messages. To do this, go to your inbox, then pull the screen down using your finger. When you see a refresh button appear, let go, and Gmail will see what messages haven't arrived yet.

# Delete an email

If your inbox is starting to get a bit cluttered, then it's a good idea to start clearing out the old emails that you no longer need. To delete an email, **tap and hold** on it, then tap the **trash** button at the top of the screen.

If you accidentally delete the wrong email, then you have 30 days to retrieve it from the trash. To do this, return to the main panel of Gmail where your inbox can be seen, tap the **menu** button in the top left corner, then choose **Bin**. Next, **tap and hold** on the message you wish to recover, tap the **options** button in the top right corner, choose **Move to**, then select **Primary**.

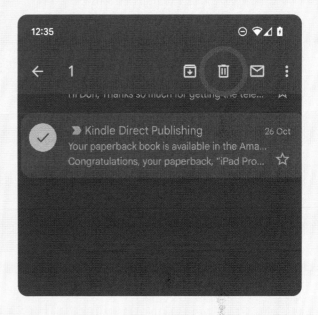

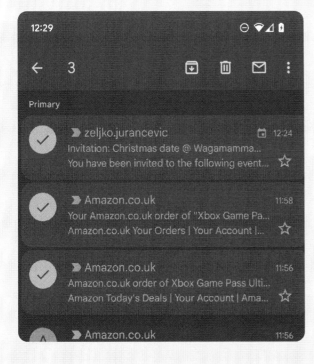

# Manage multiple emails

If you would like to delete, star, or archive multiple emails at once, then here's how it works:

1. Go to a folder of your Gmail account, such as your inbox.

2. **Tap and hold** on the first email you would like to manage. You'll see it become highlighted, and a series of buttons will appear at the top of the screen.

3. **Tap and hold** on the next message, then so on until you have selected all the emails you would like to manage.

4. Use the buttons at the top of the screen to delete, star, or archive your messages.

# Make phone calls

## Let's take a look at some phone-related tips...

The word smartphone might include the word "phone" in its name, but that doesn't mean it's used primarily as a telephone. Instead, the majority of people use their Android phones as a fully fledged computers for sharing media, browsing the web, and playing games.

Nevertheless, the Phone app is still an essential feature. One that's simple to use but with a handful of useful features. Let's take a look at them:

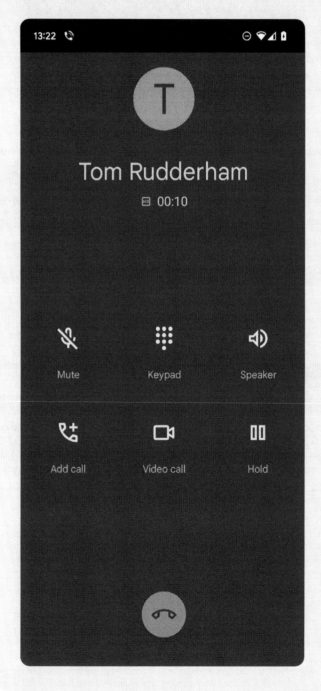

## Make a phone call

To make a call, open the Phone app, select one of your contacts, then tap the **Call** button. If you'd rather dial a number, then tap the **Keypad** button at the bottom of the screen, enter the phone number, then tap the **Call** button. You will see the screen turn dark, and a number of controls appear:

- **Mute**: Turn the microphone off, so the other person can't hear you.

- **Keypad**: Display the keypad. This is particularly helpful if you're phoning a call centre and need to enter numbers to reach the correct department.

- **Speaker**: Tap this to play audio through the phone's speakers, or to a pair of headphones.

- **Add call**: Add another person to the phone call, in effect turning it into a group call.

- **Video call:** Make a video call to the other person.

- **Hold**: Put the other person on hold while you do something else. While on hold, they will hear an intermittent beep every few seconds.

While you're making a phone call, you can go to the home screen and open other apps, all while being in a call. To return to the call, tap the **call** button in the top left corner.

When you're ready to hang up, press the **red button** at the bottom of the screen.

# Phone call tips

## If using the speaker...

Don't hold the phone to your ear. Instead, keep it at arm's length.

## Lock your phone

During a call, you can lock your phone by pressing the **power** button. This won't end your call, but it will prevent you from accidentally pressing any buttons, and it saves a bit of battery too.

## When making a call...

Make sure the phone is pressed against your face. The phone will know and deactivate the on-screen buttons, so you don't accidentally hang up using your cheek.

## Hearing aids

Many hearing aids work with Bluetooth and can be connected to your phone.

## Disconnected calls

If you hear an audio alert during the call, such as a beep, then the call might have been dropped due to a bad signal. You can double-check by looking at the screen.

## If you can't make a call...

Make sure there's a signal. To do this, look for the signal strength icon at the top of the screen.

## Recieve a call

When someone calls you several things can happen:
- The phone plays a ringtone.
- The phone vibrates.
- The touchscreen lights up and shows the incoming call.

To answer the call, swipe the screen upwards. You'll then see the phone screen as seen back across the page.

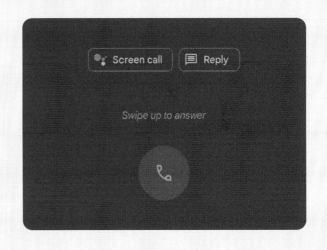

## Reject a call

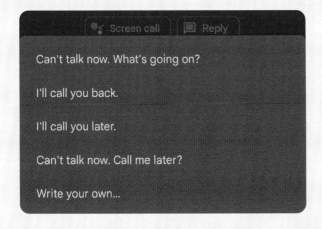

If you don't want to talk to someone, then there are a few options:
- **Ignore the call.** You can silence the ringtone by pressing the phone's volume button.
- **Dismiss the call.** You can instantly shut it up by swiping downwards.
- **Reply with a text message.** To do this, tap the **Reply** button, then either choose a stock reply or enter your own.

# Make an emergency call

If you are unable to unlock your phone and need to make an emergency call, then tap the **EMERGENCY CALL** button on the lock screen. If you don't see it straight away then swipe upwards. You can then call the emergency services in your area.

# Check your voicemail

To quickly listen to your voicemail, open the **Phone** app, tap the **keypad**, then **tap and hold** on number **1**. Your phone will then instantly dial voicemail and play back any messages that are waiting for you.

# Receive a call when you're already in a call

If you're quite a popular person and spend a lot of time on the phone, then at some point, you're going to receive a call while you're already talking to someone. If this happens, you have a number of choices:

- **Answer the call.** Swipe upwards to accept the new call. The current call will be placed on hold.
- **Send the incoming call to voicemail.**
- **Do nothing.** Eventually, the other caller will hang up and move on with their day.

If you do accept the second call, then a number of further options will become available:

- **Switch calls.** You can swap between callers by tapping the **Switch Calls** icon.
- **Merge calls.** You can combine both calls into a conference call, enabling everyone to talk to each other.

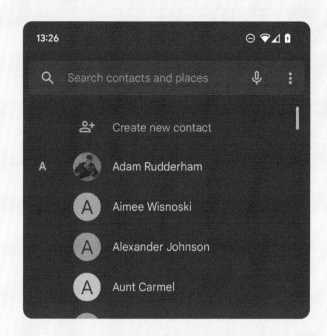

# View your contacts

The Phone app also contains all of your contact details. Think of it as a phone book and you'll get the idea. To access all of your contacts, open the Phone app then tap **Contacts** at the bottom of the screen.

To search for contact, use the **search bar** at the top of the screen and then enter someone's name or phone number.

To select a contact, simply tap on them from within the list. You can then call them, send a text message, make a video call, get directions to their address, and see their details.

# Create a new contact

To add someone new to your contacts list, open the Phone app, select **Contacts** at the bottom of the screen, then tap the **Create new contact** link at the top of the screen.

On the following screen, you can add as much information as you like, such as the person's name, number, address, title, company, and relationship. When you've finished adding details, tap the **Save** button in the top corner.

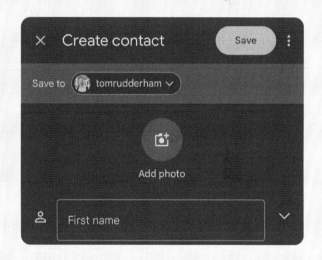

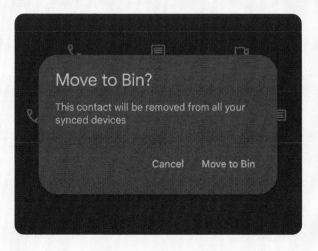

# Delete a contact

If you no longer need to stay in touch with someone, then here's how to remove their details from your phone:

1. Open the **Phone** app and tap **Contacts**.

2. Select the contact you wish to delete, then tap the **options** button in the top right corner.

3. Tap **Delete**, then in the pop-up window, confirm by tapping **Move to Bin.**

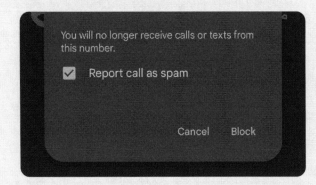

# Block numbers

To block a specific number from calling you, open the **Phone** app, select **Recents**, then **tap and hold** on the number you wish to block. Next, select **Block/report spam**, then in the pop-up window tap **Block**.

# Add a photo to a contact

1. Open the **Phone** app and tap **Contacts**.

2. Select the contact you wish to add a photo to, then tap **Edit contact**.

3. Tap **Add photo**, then either take a photo on the spot or choose one from your library.

4. Adjust the image to make sure their face is large enough to see, tap **Done**, then tap **Save**. Now, when that person calls you, you'll see their face on your phone's screen.

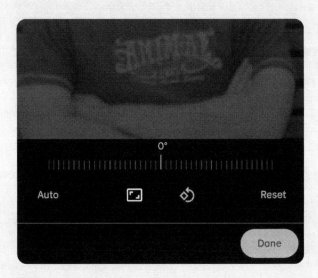

# Favourite someone

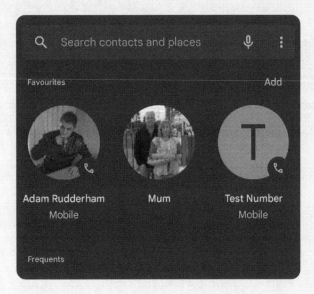

If you regularly call someone, then it's a good idea to save them as a Favourite. Once you do this, you can quickly find them by opening the Phone app, then tapping **Favourites** at the bottom of the screen.

To favourite someone, open the **Phone** app, tap **Contacts,** then select someone. Next, tap the **star** button in the top corner.

To find your Favourites list, open the **Phone** app and select **Favourites**.

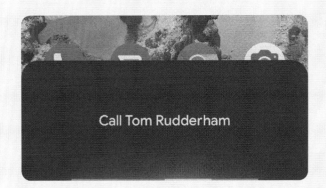

Call Tom Rudderham

# Call someone with Google Assistant

If you'd rather dictate a number than tap each key, open Google Assistant by holding the **Power** button, then say "*Call...*" followed by the number or contact name. Google Assistant will then dial the contact automatically.

# Automatically block spam calls

You can ask your phone to automatically filter spam calls and prevent them from disturbing you. To do this:

**1** Open the **Phone** app and tap the **options** button to the right of the search bar.

**2** Select **Settings**, then tap **Caller ID and spam**.

**3** Toggle **Filter spam calls** on.

# Ask your phone to read out a caller name's

If you struggle to see the text on your phone's screen, then you can ask your Android to speak out loud the caller's name and number when an incoming call arrives. To do this:

**1** Open the **Phone** app and tap the **options** button to the right of the search bar.

**2** Select **Settings**, then scroll down to the ADVANCED area.

**3** Tap **Caller ID announcement**, then tap **Announce caller ID**.

**4** In the pop-up window, select **Always**. Now, when a call arrives, you'll hear the name and number read out loud.

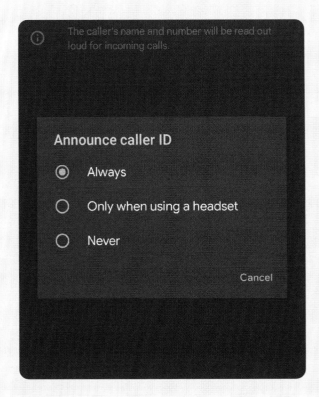

# Manage your contacts

## Add people you know and tidy up your contacts books...

While the Phone app includes the ability to add and remove contacts, there's a dedicated Contacts app installed on your smartphone, which has a few more helpful features, such as the ability to automatically update contacts details, tag people, and even jump between multiple Google accounts.

## Explore your contacts

**1** Open the **Contacts app**.

**2** You'll see a list of your contacts that scroll down the screen. Scroll through them, or use the **search** bar at the top of the screen to quickly find someone.

**3** Tap on a contact to call them, send a text message, or start a video call.

## Sort contacts

By default, the Contacts app will sort and display people by their first name. If you'd rather sort them by surname, then tap on your **profile photo** in the top right corner, choose **Contacts app settings**, then tap **Sort by**. You can then make a choice using the pop-up panel.

## Import numbers from your SIM card

If you've transferred your old SIM card to your new phone, then it's possible to automatically import all the numbers you had saved on your old phone. To do this, tap on your **profile photo** in the top right corner, choose **Contacts app settings**, then tap **Import**. Next, select **SIM card**, then tap **OK**.

# Assign a custom ringtone to someone

If you're regularly in touch with someone, then it's a good idea to give them a unique ringtone. By doing this you'll know who's calling before you even look at the screen. To do this:

**1** Open the **Contacts app** and select a contact.

**2** Tap the **options** button in the top right corner, then choose **Set ringtone**.

**3** Scroll through the list and tap on each ringtone to preview it.

**4** Once you find a ringtone that you like, tap **SAVE** in the top right corner.

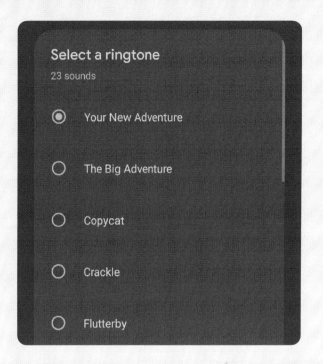

# Merge and fix duplicate contacts

If you've had your phone for some time, or upgraded from one phone to another, then you might start to collect duplicate contacts, old phone numbers, and out of date details. Your phone can attempt to automatically merge duplicates, and update details from people's Google accounts on the internet. To do this:

**1** Open the **Contacts app** and tap the **menu** button in the top left corner.

**2** Tap **Merge and fix**.

**3** Your phone will look for any fixes and updates, hen offer you multiple options. Here are a couple of examples:

- **Keep contacts up to date.** This will automatically fix and merge any out of date contacts.

- **Add people you email often.** This option will look through your Google email account, and add contacts that you regularly get in touch with.

# Make a video call

## Make a free video call to friends and family using Duo...

With the Duo app on your phone, you can be with friends and family at any time and place. Whether it's a birthday, anniversary, meeting, or just a chat, Duo lets you be a part of the moment with crystal clear video and audio. Duo works over Wi-Fi, and enables you to call anyone else with a smartphone. If the recipient doesn't have Duo (for example, they have an iPhone or iPad), then you can invite them to download the Duo app (it's free), and then video call for free.

You'll find the Duo app already installed on your Android. To find it, just tap on this icon:

## Make a video call

To start a video call with someone, open the **Duo** app, then tap **New Call**. On the following screen, select someone from your contacts, then tap **Video call**. While you wait for them to answer, you can send a number of emojis (such as wave, heart, and thumbs up), by tapping on the icons near the top of the screen. These will appear as a notification on the other person's phone or computer.

## During a call...

1. Tap on your preview video to view it full size. You can also slide it around the screen.

2. Tap this button to take a photo of the current video call.

3. If you need a moment of privacy, tap this button to turn off your video.

4. Similarly, you can mute yourself with this button.

5. End the call by tapping the red button.

6. Swap to the back-facing camera or back again.

7. Add a number of crazy video effects. See across the page for more on this.

# Add a video effect

If you'd like to add some humour to a video call, try replacing your outfit with something that's totally out there, such as a pirates suit or a chicken costume. Here's how it works:

**1** During a call, tap the **effects** button at the bottom of the screen.

**2** Tap **Effects**. You'll see thumbnails appear along the bottom of the screen. Tap on one to select it, then look at your image to see how you appear.

**3** To blur your background, tap **Portrait**.

**4** To keep the kids entertained during a video call, tap **Family**. This will enable children to add their own effects or draw on the screen using their finger.

# Make a group call

With support for up to 32 people at once, making a group Duo group call is a great way to communicate with friends, family and work colleagues. Here's how it works:

**1** Open the **Duo** app, then tap **New call** in the bottom corner.

**2** Tap **Create Group**.

**3** Select the contacts you wish to invite to the group call, then tap **Done**.

**4** To share the link with your contacts, tap the **share** button, then send the link via Messages, Gmail, or any social media apps you have installed.

- If the recipient clicks the link on a computer, it opens duo.google.com.
- If the recipient taps the link on mobile and Duo is installed, the Google Duo app opens.
- If the recipient taps the link on mobile and Duo isn't installed, the link opens Google Duo in Google Play or the App Store.

# Tips for making a great video call:

✓ Make sure the other person can see you. It's easy to forget where the camera is pointing, so use the small preview image to check your appearance.

✓ The microphone is located on the bottom of your phone, so if the other person says they can't hear you, make sure your fingers aren't covering the bottom of the device.

✓ If you turn your Android on its side during a call, the other person will see more of the room around you.

# Manage your calendar

## Learn how to add events and manage multiple calendars...

The calendar app on your Android is surprisingly powerful. It can juggle multiple events throughout your day, factor in the time it takes to travel from one event to another, and even automatically block out chunks of time when you're on the road. It's also the place where you can add upcoming reminders.

To find the Calendar app, simply search for it or look for this icon:

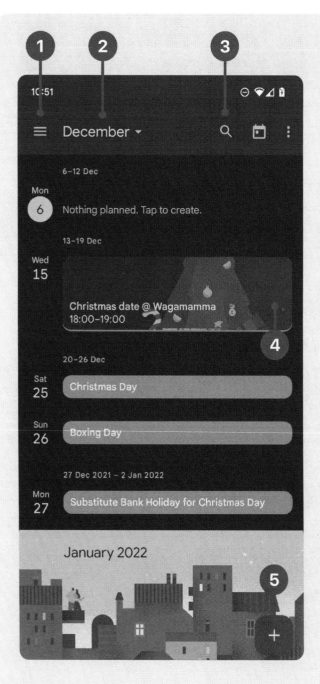

## The basics

1. Tap the **menu** button to jump between views or toggle settings.

2. See an overview of the entire month by tapping this button.

3. Search for a specific calendar event, date, or reminder.

4. Tap on an event to see more details, or swipe across it to delete it.

5. Add a new calendar event by tapping this button.

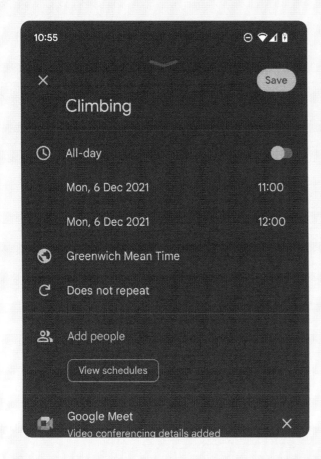

# Add a calendar event

**1** Tap the **plus** button in the bottom-right corner, then choose to add a goal, reminder, task, or event.

**2** Give the event a name by tapping on **Add title**.

**3** Choose a date and time using the controls below the title.

**4** If you'd like to invite someone else, then tap **Add people** and enter a name from your contacts list.

**5** If you're setting up a video call, then tap **Add video conferencing**, and your phone will automatically add a link to Google Meet.

**6** If the event takes place at a location, then tap the grey **Location** text to search for a place.

**7** Tap the **Save** button when you're ready to add the event to your calendar.

# See the month ahead

Tap the name of the month at the top of the screen and you'll see an overview of the month ahead. If you see a dot on one of the days then there's an event in your calendar.

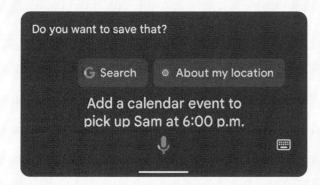

# Add an event with Google Assistant

To quickly add an event to your calendar, initiate Google Assistant by holding down the **power** button, then say something like "*add a calendar event to pick up Sam at 6 PM*".

# Add a reminder

If you need to do something later in the day (or on a specific day), then here's how to add a reminder:

**1** Tap the **plus** button in the bottom-right corner, then choose **Reminder**.

**2** Give the reminder a name by tapping on **Remind me to…**

**3** If your reminder is later in the day, untoggle **All-day,** then select a time by tapping on the **time**.

**4** To change the day of the reminder, tap on the **date**, then use the calendar to pick a date.

**5** If you'd like to repeat your reminder every day, week, month, or year, then tap **Does not repeat** and select an option.

**6** Tap **Save** when you're ready to add your event to your calendar.

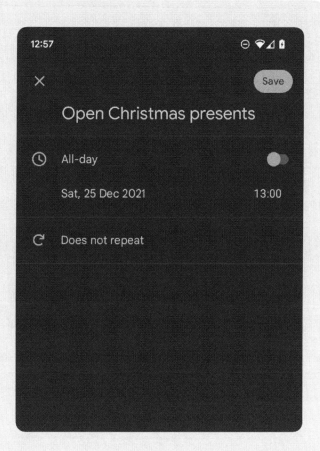

# Get automatic alerts

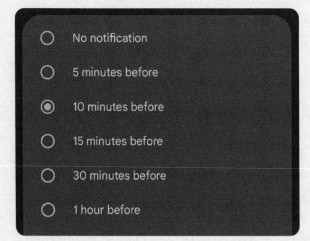

By default, the calendar app will remind you of events 10 minutes before they happen. If you'd like to customise this and be reminded an hour, a day, or longer beforehand, then:

**1** Tap the **menu** button in the top left corner, then select **Events**.

**2** Under **Default notifications**, tap on **10 minutes before**, then make a selection using the pop-up window.

# Quickly delete an event

Swipe from left to right across an event, then tap the **Trash** button which appears.

# Search for an event

If you have a busy calendar ahead and don't have time to manually look for a specific event, simply use the **search bar** at the top of the screen and enter an event name, date, or time.

# Toggle calendar views

The default calendar view will show a highlighted version of your schedule ahead, but if you have a busy calendar, then it might be easier to see the week or day ahead. To do this:

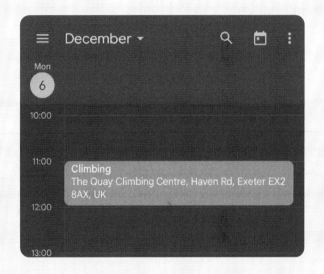

1. Tap the **menu** button in the top left corner.

2. Choose **Day** to see the day ahead, **3 days** to see the next three days, or **week** or **month**.

3. To return to the default view, tap the **menu** button then choose **Schedule**.

# Switch to light view

By default, the Calendar app will appear dark with highlighted events and text. To switch to a light version, where the background appears white:

1. Tap the **menu** button in the top left corner, then select **Settings**.

2. Choose **General,** then scroll down and tap **Theme**.

3. In the pop-up window, make a choice and you'll see the app instantly switch over.

# Capture photo or video

## Get to know the camera app and all of its features...

Smartphones dominate the camera industry. Take a look at Flickr and you'll see that smartphones are by far the most popular type of camera, heavily overtaking traditional brands such as Canon and Nikon. Over recent years, the camera app within your smartphone has become ever more advanced, until today it's able to recognise faces, analyse lighting conditions, record slow-motion video, and much more. As a result, the Android in your pocket is capable of taking truly beautiful photos.

To find the Camera app, just look for this icon:

## The basics

1. Tap the **settings** button to adjust individual settings for each camera mode.

2. Jump to your Photo Gallery.

3. This is a level meter. It lets you know when the camera is aligned with the horizon. When it says 0°, you're perfectly aligned.

4. If your camera has multiple lenses, then you can toggle between them using these shortcuts.

5. Tap the large **white shutter** button to take a photo.

6. Flip between forward and back cameras.

7. Open the most recently snapped photo by tapping this button.

8. Toggle between camera modes by using these shortcuts. There might be more than what you see on the screen, depending on the cameras your phone has and its version of Android. To explore more camera modes, swipe through these shortcuts by sliding them left or right.

# Use the volume buttons

It's possible to take a photo by pressing the **volume up or down** buttons on the side of your phone. This is especially useful for taking selfies with your arm outstretched.

# Zoom even further

You can manually zoom the camera lens by pinching two fingers on the screen and then pulling them apart. Depending on your phone's camera system, you might be able to zoom anywhere between 2X and 100X.

As you zoom in, notice the slider below the image preview. This also lets you control the zoom level by sliding it left and right.

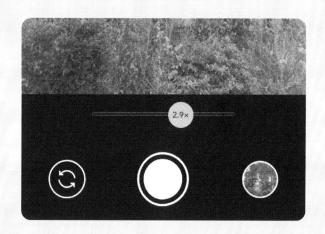

# Focus the camera

The camera will automatically focus onto a prominent object or area of light, but if you need to manually focus the camera, just tap on the area or subject you wish to focus on.

After tapping on an area, you'll see the outline of a white circle appear. You'll also see a number of slider controls appear:

- **Brightness**: Slide this left or right to adjust the brightness of the photo.
- **Contrast**: Use this to adjust the contrast.
- **Temperature hue**: Use this to make the image appear warmer or colder.

# Access additional settings

Notice the settings button in the top left corner of the screen. You can tap on this to access additional settings, for example when set to the **Video** mode, you can tap **settings** to toggle the flash, adjust video resolution, and frame rate.

# Take a Portrait photo

If you have one of the latest Android phones, then it's possible to take a Portrait photo, where the background behind the subject is blurred with a natural-looking effect. To do this, open the **Camera** app and then tap on the **Portrait** button at the bottom of the screen. Next, use either the front or back-facing camera to take a photo of yourself, someone else, or even an object.

# Capture a Time Lapse

Have you ever wanted to capture a sun set, the changing tides, or the movement of clouds? Using the Camera app you can do this with the time-lapse feature. It works by capturing multiple photos, instead of video, over a period of time.

To capture a time-lapse video, open the **Camera** app, select the **Video** mode, then select **Time Lapse**. Next, place your phone in a suitable location. Make sure it's steady – any movements over time will ruin the time-lapse effect. When you're ready, tap the **shutter** button. Leave your Android for a few moments or minutes - the longer the better as you'll capture more footage - then tap the red shutter button to end the time-lapse.

# Film in slow motion

One of the most fun features included with the Camera app is the ability to shoot video in slow motion at either 1/8th of the usual speed, or 1/4th. This is great for capturing fast-moving objects or subjects, such as someone jumping in the air or a vehicle whizzing by.

To capture a time-lapse video, open the **Camera** app, select the **Video** mode, then select **Slow Motion**. When you're ready, tap the **shutter** button to begin recording, capture the person or object in front of you, then tap the red **shutter** button to stop filming. You can now watch your video back by tapping on the **thumbnail** in the lower right corner.

# Use Action Pan to add a creative blur

The latest Android phones are powerful enough to capture fast-moving objects and then add an artificial blur to the background, effectively giving them a cinematic appearance. To use this mode:

1 Open the **Camera** app, then select **Motion**.

2 Make sure **Action pan** is enabled.

3 When you're ready, tap the **shutter** button, then keep the moving object or person in focus as they pass by in front of you.

4 When you're finished capturing the moment, tap the red **shutter** button. You can then watch your Action Pan video back by tapping the **thumbnail** in the lower right corner.

91

# Take a long exposure photo

Another feature shared by the latest Android phones is the ability to take a long exposure photo. It works by blurring any movement taken during a five-second exposure, so if you take a photo of running water, it will appear transparent and ethereal, or if you take a photo of a passing train, it will appear as a blurry streak. To capture a long exposure photo:

1. Open the **Camera** app, then select **Motion**.

2. Tap on **Long exposure**.

3. When you're ready, tap the **shutter** button, then hold your phone as still as possible.

4. When you're finished capturing the moment, tap the **shutter** button. You can now view your long exposure photo by tapping the **thumbnail** in the lower right corner. You can compare it with a normal photo (taken at the same time) by swiping the image to the left.

# Capture a panoramic shot

Have you ever wanted to capture an incredibly beautiful vista? By using the Panorama mode you can do just this by taking a super-wide, 180-degree photo. Here's how it works:

1. Open the **Camera** app, then select **Modes**.

2. Tap on **Panorama**.

3. When you're ready, tap the **shutter** button, then slowly pan your device to the right. Keep a steady hand - if you wobble too much black bars will appear at the top and bottom of the photo.

4. When you're finished capturing the moment, tap the **shutter** button. You can now view your panoramic photo by tapping the **thumbnail** in the lower right corner.

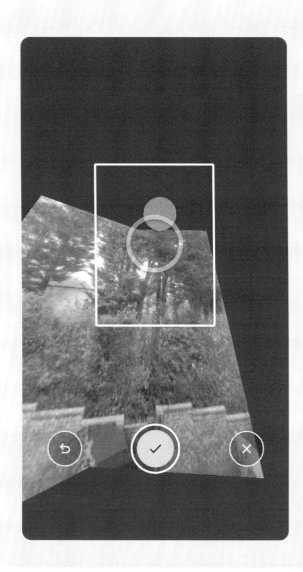

# Capture a 3D sphere of the environment

The Camera app on your Android has a unique way of capturing the room or environment around you: it can take dozens of photos to create a 3D sphere that you can later explore. Here's how it works:

1. Open the **Camera** app, then select **Modes**.

2. Tap on **Photo Sphere**.

3. To begin capturing the environment, tap the **shutter** button, then centre the blue dot inside the rectangle by moving your phone. Hold still, and the first photo will be taken.

4. Next, move your phone to the edges of the rectangle until you see another blue dot appear. Centre this dot and keep still.

5. Keep capturing photos of the environment around you by moving your phone and taking photos, until you've captured enough. When you're finished, tap the **tick** button.

6. You can now view your 3D sphere photo by tapping the **thumbnail** in the lower right corner.

# Take photos in the dark

Night Sight mode combines long exposure and clever computational software, to capture as much light as possible in the dark. It works automatically, so all you need to do is press the shutter button and keep your phone as still as possible:

1. Open the **Camera** app, then select **Night Sight**. If you don't see it, scroll the shortcuts at the bottom of the screen to the left.

2. Tap the **shutter** button, then hold your phone as still as possible. If it's very dark then you might have to wait a while for the camera to capture as much light as possible.

3. 

4. When the photo has been taken, tap the **thumbnail** button to view it.

# View and edit your Photos

## Learn how to view, organise, and edit your photos...

The Photos app is a portal to your memories. Stored within its colourful icon are hundreds, if not thousands of treasured photos and videos. Photos of yapping dogs, family members, stunning landscapes, unflattering selfies, and treasured holidays. This is one of those apps that you're going to be opening on a day-to-day basis, so keep it somewhere prominent on the Home Screen where you can easily find it.

To find the Photos app, look for the colourful flower icon:

## The basics

1. Ever wanted to print your own photo book? Tap this button and Google will offer you a selection of options.

2. Tap on your **profile photo** to access settings and see how much storage data you have remaining.

3. This scrubber button enables you to quickly scrub through your entire photo library by sliding your finger up and down the screen.

4. Tap on a photo to instantly open it.

5. This shortcut button brings you back to the main view of the Photos app (as seen here).

6. Tap **Search** to look for people, objects, and things within photos.

7. If you have shared photos or albumbs with other people - or vice versa - then you can access your shared content by tapping this button.

8. Access all of the albums on your phone by tapping this button, plus your favourite images and the Bin.

# Basics of viewing photos

After opening the Photos app, simply tap on the thumbail of an image to view it full screen. You can zoom further by pinching on the screen with two fingers, and rotate your phone on its side to get a better view.

# Find out more about an object, animal, or location

One of the most impressive features of the Photos app is its ability to recognise something, then give you more information about it. For example, you can open a photo of a cat and then find out its breed. You can open a photo of a landmark and find out where it is, and see photos other people have taken. You can even take photos of artwork and find out who created it. Here's how it works:

1. Open the **Photos** app, then open an image.

2. Tap on the **Lens** button at the bottom of the screen. If you don't see it then you might have an older Android phone that doesn't support this feature.

3. After tapping lens, wait a moment for your phone to scan the image and look on the internet for more details. After a moment or two, you'll see this information appear below the photo.

4. To learn more about the subject matter in the photo, scroll down to see results from Google.

5. If there's text in the photo, then you can translate it between languages by tapping **Translate**.

6. If you're interested in purchasing something in a photo, then tap **Shopping**.

# Search your photos

The Photos app can recognise objects, faces and places, then automatically organise groups of images into albums for you to enjoy. This clever form of visual recognition has another benefit: intelligent searching. To search for something in an image, tap the **Search** button at the bottom of the screen.

Search for *"California"* and you'll see all your photos of California. You can be even more specific. So search for *"Trees in California"* and the Photos app will automatically show photos of trees within California. You can try other queries such as *"Tom eating pizza"*, or *"Sarah riding a horse"* and the app will instantly present you with results.

# View categories and types of photos

The Photos app will automatically categorise your images by type and media. For example, it will put selfies into a category called (you guessed it), Selfies. Videos go into Videos, and so on.

To find and explore these categories, open the Photos app and tap on **Search** at the bottom of the screen. Next, scroll down and you'll see the Categories panel appear.

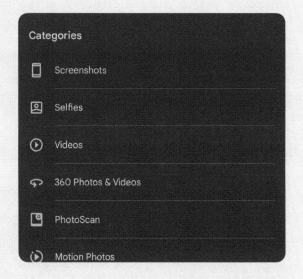

# Favourite an image

If there's a photo that you particularly love, and want to revisit in the future, then open it and tap the **Star** button in the upper right corner.

To find your favourited images, tap **Library** at the bottom of the screen, then tap **Favourites**.

# Create an album

If you would like to organise your photos into albums, then the Photos app makes this nice and simple:

**1** Open the **Photos** app, then tap the **Library** button at the bottom of the screen.

**2** Scroll down slightly, and you'll see a section called Albums.

**3** Tap **New album**, then on the following screen, give it a title.

**4** To start adding photos from your library, tap **Select photos**, then tap on the images you wish to add into the new album. Tap **Add** in the top right corner when you've finished. Your new album is ready to view and share with others.

# Rename an album

To change the name of an album, simply open it and then tap on the **title** at the top of the screen. Use the keyboard to edit the name, and then tap the **tick** button in the upper left corner to save your changes.

# Delete an album

If you're fed up of an album, open it, tap the **options** button in the upper right corner, and then choose **Delete album**. In the pop-up window, confirm your choice by selecting **Delete**, and the album will be removed from your phone and Google Photos account.

Keep in mind that it's only the album that is deleted. Any photos and videos inside will still remain on your phone. You can find them by tapping Photos at the bottom of the screen.

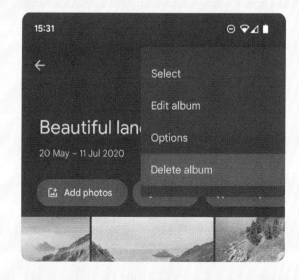

# Share a photo or video

Open an image or video, then tap the **Share** button in the bottom left corner.

You'll see the share panel slide up the screen. You can send a photo or video to a contact at the top of the panel, or send it via Gmail, Messages, and more using the shortcut buttons below.

# Edit a photo

Want to improve the look of a photo you've taken on your phone? Begin by selecting an image in the Photos app, then tap the **Edit** button at the bottom of the screen. You'll then see a number of editing tools appear:

1. These large buttons are filters that can dramatically change how an image appears. Try them out by selecting one at a time. You can find more by scrolling the filters towards the left.

2. These shortcuts at the bottom enable you to crop an image, adjust its appearance, or add text and annotations.

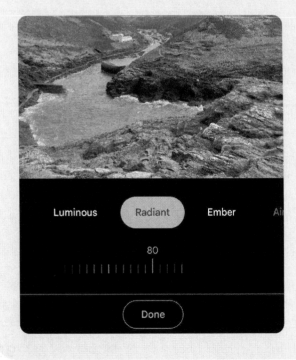

# Quickly adjust the sky

If you've taken a photo of an overcast day, then it's possible to adjust the image to make it look sunnier, stormy, radiant, and much more. To do this:

1. Open the image, then tap **Edit**.

2. Scroll through the shortcuts at the bottom of the screen, then choose **Tools**.

3. Tap **Sky**, then make a selection using the presets provided by Google. You can adjust the strength of the effect by dragging the slider at the bottom of the screen.

4. Tap **Save copy** when you've finished making changes.

# Erase small objects, blemishes and marks

If you'd like to remove an imperfection in a photo, such as a mark, scratch, small object, or even a person in the background, then here's what to do:

1. Open the image, then tap **Edit**.

2. Scroll through the shortcuts at the bottom of the screen, then choose **Tools**.

3. Tap **Magic Eraser.** Zoom into the object or area that you would like to erase using two fingers.

4. Rub your finger over the object or area that you would like to delete. When you let go, your phone will attempt to magically erase it.

5. If you're happy with the result, tap **Save copy** to finish making changes. If the magic eraser doesn't quite do the job, then tap the **back arrow** to try again, or **Reset** to stop making changes.

# Crop or rotate an image

While editing a photo, tap the **Crop** button at the bottom of the screen. To crop a photo, drag the edges of the photo inwards. If you crop too much, then you can pinch on the image with two fingers to zoom out.

To rotate an image, drag the **horizontal slider** at the bottom of the screen. As you drag it left or right, you'll see the photo above rotate. A thin grid of lines will also appear, which is helpful for aligning objects or the horizon.

Tap **Save copy** when you've finished making changes.

# Manually adjust an image

The Photos app includes a suite of tools for manually adjusting an image. For example, you can tweak the brightness of contrast, apply a HDR effect, or adjust the white point and highlights. Here's how it works:

1. Open the image, then tap **Edit**.

2. Scroll through the shortcuts at the bottom of the screen, then choose **Tools**.

3. Tap **Adjust**, then make a selection using the tools that appear above. You can adjust the strength of a tool by dragging the slider at the bottom of the screen.

4. Tap **Save copy** when you've finished making changes.

# Apply a filter

Filters are great for quickly adjusting the overall appearance of a photo. There are 13 included within the Photos app, enabling you to instantly turn an image into an evocative-looking shot. To apply a filter:

1. Open the image, then tap **Edit**.

2. Scroll through the shortcuts at the bottom of the screen, then choose **Filters**.

3. Tap on a filter to instantly apply it to the photo. You can scroll the filters towards the left to find more.

4. Tap **Save copy** when you've finished making changes.

# See where a photo was taken

Whenever you take a photo with a smartphone or modern DSLR, the location it was taken at will be saved within its EXIF data. This means you can see where the photo was taken on a map using the Photos app. To do this:

1. Open the image, then tap the **options** button in the top right corner. It looks like three dots.

2. Scroll the pop-up panel upwards, and you'll see a map view appear.

3. Tap on this map to open the location within the Google Maps app.

# Order a printed book of images from Google

Using the Photos app, it's possible to create a softcover or hardcover photo book to share your memories. This will later arrive in the post, and it makes for a great gift for someone. To do this:

1. Open the **Photos** app, then tap the **Photo books** button in the top left corner. It looks like a small shopping bag.

2. Tap **Make a photo book** at the bottom of the screen.

3. Select at least 20 photos. If you select more than 140 photos, some of your photos will be collaged in one page.

4. Tap **Done**, and your photo book will be saved automatically. You can then follow the on-screen instructions to design the cover and spine, layout, and book type. You'll also be asked to pay for the book using the payment details saved in your Google account.

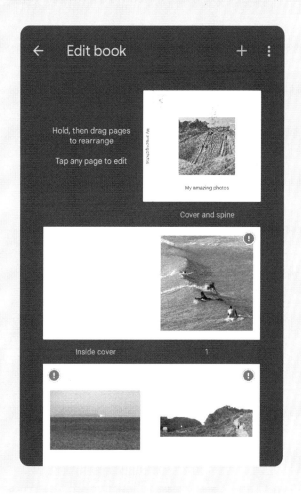

# Listen to YouTube Music

## Listen to your favourite tracks and albums on Apple Music...

There's no default music player app on your Android phone, but it should come with YouTube Music. Think of YouTube Music as a portal to nearly every single, album, and artist you can think of. Alongside more than 70 million official songs, it also includes live performances, covers, and remixes.

To access the full service, you'll need to pay a monthly subscription. It's priced slightly differently for each country but roughly works out about the same as a large takeaway pizza. To find the YouTube Music app on your phone, open the App Drawer and look for "YT Music". If you don't see it, then you can open the Google Play app, search for "YouTube Music", and download the app for free.

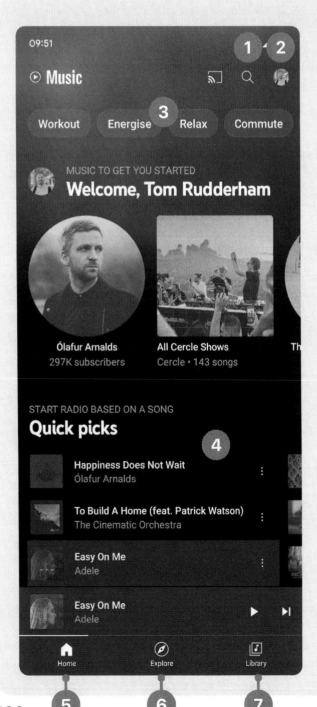

## Explore YouTube Music

Open the YouTube Music app and you'll first see the Home screen. Here's a quick overview of what to expect:

**1** Tap the **search** button to look for tracks, albums, artists, and music videos.

**2** Tap on your **profile photo** to access settings, see your listening history, and access any downloads.

**3** These listening suggestions will change depending on your listening history and the time of day. Tap on one to explore a variety of music based on the suggestion.

**4** Scroll down to explore music suggestions. You'll find radio stations based on songs and artists, playlist mixes, hits, and more.

**5** You can get back to this screen at any time by tapping the **Home** shortcut.

**6** Tap **Explore** to check out the latest releases, top charts, music genres, and music videos.

**7** Tap **Library** to see your recent listening activity, downloads, playlists, albums, songs, artists and subscriptions.

# Search for music

If you're looking for an artist, song, album, or even lyrics, then tap the **Search** button at the top of the screen. Start to type the name of an artist, song, or album, and suggestions will appear below. Tap on one to start playing it.

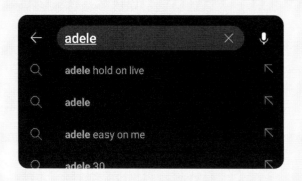

# Control music playback

Here are the basic playback controls when listening to music in the YouTube Music app:

1. If there's a music video available for a song, then tap the **Video** tab at the top of the screen to watch it.

2. Tap the **down arrow** to minimise the playback panel. You can then continue to explore the YouTube Music app.

3. Tap the **options** button to start a radio station based upon the song playing, add a song to your library, download it, add it to a playlist, or jump to the full album or artists page.

4. Rate a song to let YouTube Music know if you like it or not. If you give a song the thumbs up, the app will suggest more music like it in the future.

5. Scrub through a song by dragging the small white dot along the timeline.

6. Shuffle the songs within an album.

7. Play a song on repeat.

8. See what tracks are coming up next in an album.

9. View the lyrics for a song.

10. See similar music to the track you're currently listening to.

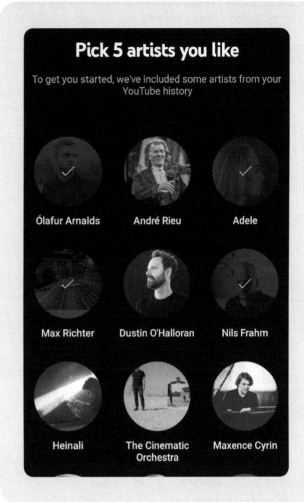

# Tell YouTube Music what you like

By telling YouTube Music who your favourite artists are, you'll receive better music recommendations and playlists. To do this:

**1** Open YouTube Music, then tap **Home** at the bottom of the screen.

**2** Scroll down and look for the **Tell us which artists you like** panel, then tap **LET'S GO**.

**3** The app will try to guess which artists you like by looking through your listening history, then suggest them on the screen. Tap on five artists that you like. As you tap each one, similar artists will pop into view. Feel free to tap on any of these that you also like.

**4** Tap **FINISHED** when you've tapped at least five artists. Now, when you explore the YouTube Music app, you'll see more personalised recommendations.

# Add music to your library

While listening to an album, tap the **plus** button alongside the album artwork to add the entire album to your library.

If you're listening to a song, tap the **options** button in the upper right corner, then choose **Add to library** to add a single track to your library.

To find your library, tap the **Library** button at the bottom of the screen, then use the shortcuts to jump to your playlists, albums, and songs.

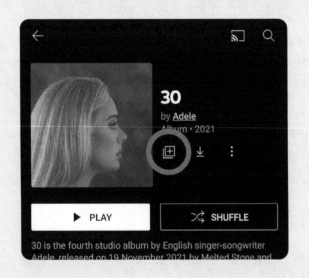

# Create a Playlist

Think of a playlist as your very own custom album, one with as many tracks and artists as you like. To create a new playlist of your own, tap **Library**, select **Playlists**, then choose **New Playlist...**

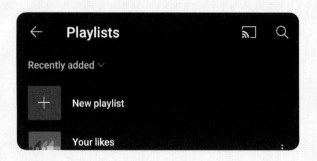

# Add music to a playlist

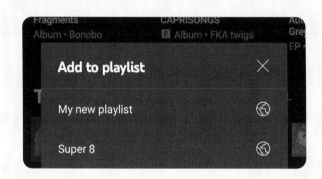

To add a track or album to your new playlist, search for it in either your music library or YouTube Music, tap the **options** button to its right, then choose **Add to playlist**. You can then choose a playlist via the pop-up window.

# Watch music videos

YouTube Music contains a wealth of music videos, covering the latest charts to pop classics. To find them, tap **Explore** at the bottom of the screen, scroll down and look for **New music videos**. Tap **SEE ALL** to explore the latest videos, or tap on a video to watch it straight away.

# See the top charts

Want to see what's number one in the charts? Tap **Explore** at the bottom of the screen, scroll down and look for **Top songs**. To listen to a track, simply tap on it.

# Shuffle music

If you're bored of an album track order, tap **Shuffle** and you'll never know what song is coming up next.

# Delete a track or album

Fed up with a song or album? Just **tap and hold** on the track name or album artwork, then tap **Remove album from Library**.

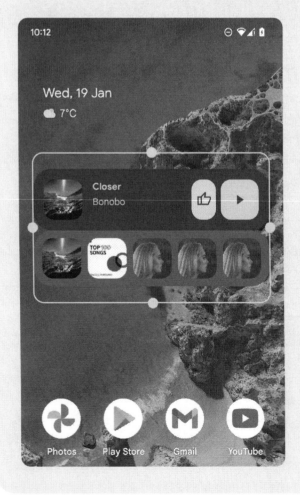

# Add a Music widget to the Home Screen

By adding a YouTube Music widget to the Home Screen, you can quickly jump to a recent song or album.

1. On the Home Screen, **tap and hold** in an empty part of the screen.

2. When the pop-up window appears, tap on **Widgets**.

3. Scroll down, then tap on **YouTube Music**. You'll see a number of widget options appear. To select one, **tap and hold** on it, then drag it to where you would like to place it on the Home Screen.

4. You can adjust the size of a widget by dragging one of the handles on its edge. When you're happy with the placement and size, tap anywhere outside of the widget, and it will lock into place.

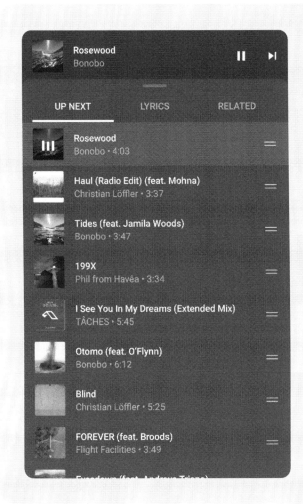

# Listen to a radio station of music you love

While listening to music on your phone, you can ask YouTube Music to create a radio station based solely on the style and genre that you're currently listening to. Here's how it works:

**1** While listening to music, tap the **options** button in the upper right corner.

**2** Choose **Start Radio**.

**3** YouTube Music will take a moment to create an endless radio station based on the music you're listening to. You can leave your phone running and the music will keep on coming.

**4** To see what's coming up next, tap **UP NEXT** at the bottom of the screen.

# See music lyrics

If you're listening to a song and it has lyrics available, tap **LYRICS** at the bottom of the screen and you'll see the full set of lyrics appear.

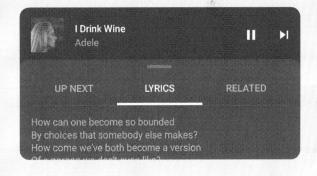

# Watch YouTube videos

## Watch an endless parade of videos, news stories, short films and more...

It's hard to understate just how important YouTube has become. Not only is it the biggest source of video content on the entire internet, but for many people, it's their primary source of video entertainment and news. More people "tune" into YouTube each day than all traditional TV channels and stations combined. Additionally, it has become the primary source of income for a large number of people who post daily content such as reaction videos, gaming videos, and reviews.

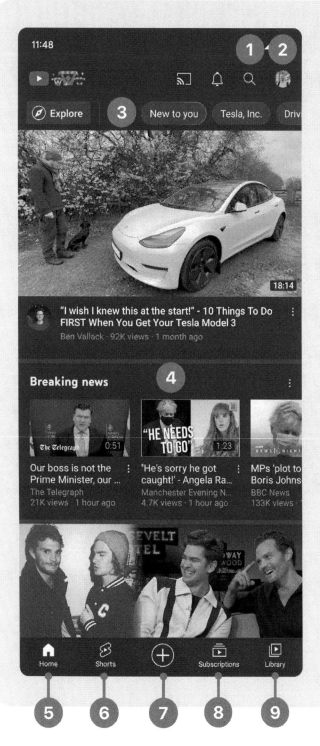

## Explore YouTube

Open the YouTube app and you'll first see the Home screen. Here's a quick overview of what to expect:

1. Tap the **search** button to (you guessed it) find videos related to nearly any subject.

2. Tap on your **profile photo** to access settings, see your viewing history, and access any downloads.

3. These video suggestions will change depending on your listening history and the time of day. Tap on one to explore a variety of videos based on the suggestion.

4. Scroll down to explore videos suggestions. These will change depending on the time of day and your viewing history. Here you can see the latest news stories.

5. You can get back to this screen at any time by tapping the **Home** shortcut.

6. Tap **Shorts** to instantly watch a random short video from YouTube. Scroll upwards to swap to the next video.

7. Tap **plus** to upload a video of your own. You can also upload a short video or start a live stream.

8. Tap **Subscriptions** to see the latest videos from any channels you subscribe to.

9. Tap **Library** to see your viewing history, downloaded videos, videos marked as Watch Later, and Playlists.

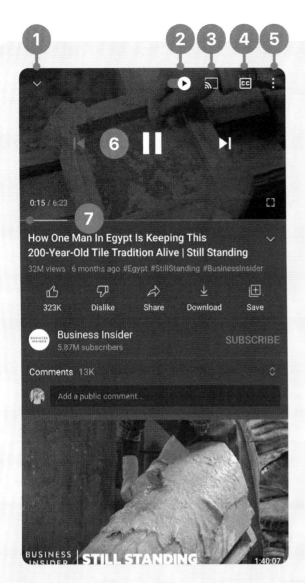

# The basics of watching a video

Start playing a video on your phone and you'll notice a small number of controls appear. Here's what each of them does:

**1** While watching a video, tap this button to minimise the video to the bottom of the screen.

**2** Tap this button to turn Auto Play off, so when the video ends, a new one won't automatically start.

**3** Tap this button to stream a video to a TV or other streaming device.

**4** Enable subtitles by tapping this button.

**5** Tap the **options** button to adjust the video quality, playback speed, or adjust the audio controls.

**6** Tap on a video while it's playing to show the playback controls.

**7** You can use this timeline to jump through a video. You can either tap on the timeline, or drag the timeline control.

# Like or dislike a video

If you're enjoying a video, tap the **thumbs up** button to like it. This lets the creator know you enjoyed the video, and also adds it to your Liked folder. To find this, tap **Library**, then choose **Liked videos**.

You can dislike a video to let the creator know, but the total number of dislikes remains hidden.

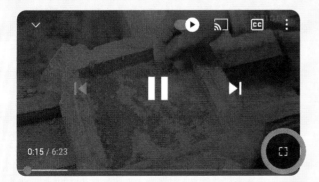

# Watch a video full screen

Watching a video full screen can be particularly helpful if your phone has a small screen, or if you're struggling to see the video.

To watch a video full screen, tap on the video while it is playing, then tap the **full screen** button in the lower right corner.

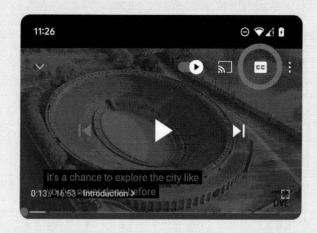

# Turn on subtitles

If you're struggling to hear the audio, or want to turn the volume right down and still follow along, then tap on the video while it's playing, then hit the **CC** button.

If a creator has not manually added subtitles, then YouTube will attempt to automatically transcribe the video for you. It works surprisingly well, even with regional accents.

# Subscribe to a channel

Content creators on YouTube typically upload new videos on a daily or weekly basis, as this encourages people to subscribe while also improving their rankings and visibility. To subscribe to a channel, tap the **SUBSCRIBE** text while watching one of their videos or while exploring their channel.

Once subscribed, you'll find the latest videos from the channel by tapping the **Subscriptions** button at the bottom of the screen.

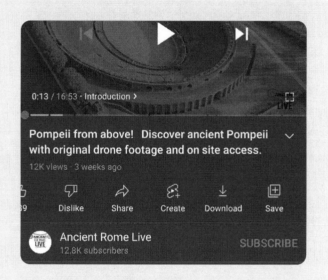

# Save a video

If you'd like to save a video, tap the **Save** button beneath the video window. This will add the video to a new playlist in your account, which you can find by tapping **Library**, then **My new playlist**.

# Watch a video later

If you're browsing YouTube and see an interesting video, but don't have time to watch it straight away, then tap the **options** button to its right, then choose **Save to Watch Later**.

When you open YouTube at a later time, you'll see the video appear at the top of the screen. You can also find it by tapping **Library**, then **Watch Later**.

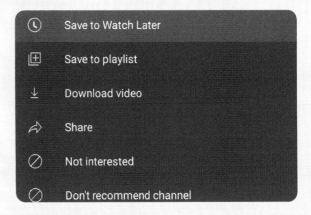

# Download a video

If you're subscribed to YouTube Premium ($11.99 / £9.99 at the time of writing), then it's possible to download a video to your smartphone. This can be particularly helpful if you're travelling on a plane or visiting an area with no signal.

To download a video, tap the **options** button to its right, then choose **Download video**. You can also start watching a video, then tap the **Download** button beneath the video window.

# Adjust the video quality

Depending on how fast your internet connection is, the video playback quality might jump from blurry to crystal clear. YouTube will attempt to automatically adjust the video quality based on your internet speed, but if you would like to manually adjust it, then:

1. While watching a video, tap the **options** button in the upper right corner.

2. Tap **Quality**.

3. **Auto** will automatically adjust the video based on your internet speed.

4. Choose **Higher picture quality** for the best image, or **Data saver** if there's not much signal. Alternatively, choose **Advanced**, then pick a resolution. The higher the number, the sharper the image.

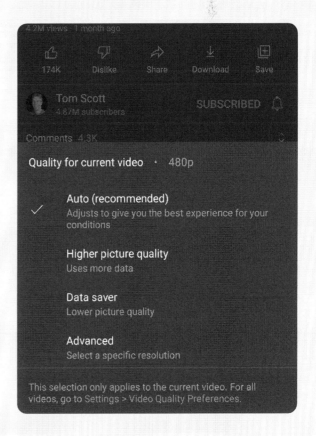

# Check notifications

Often YouTube will attempt to notify you about updates from content creators that you follow, such as live streams and new videos. You can see these notifications at any time by tapping the **bell** icon at the top of the screen.

# Upload a video of your own to YouTube

If you'd like to upload a video to YouTube and share it with the world, then here's how it works:

1. Open the YouTube app, then tap the **plus** button at the bottom of the screen.

2. Choose **Upload a video**.

3. If this is the first time you've uploaded, tap **ALLOW ACCESS**, then **Allow** in the pop-up window.

4. Choose a recent video from your phone. You'll see a preview of it begin to play. If it's the correct video tap **NEXT**.

5. Give your video a title, then add a description to help people understand the content.

6. By default, all videos uploaded to YouTube are available for everyone to see. To change this, tap **Public**, then choose **Unlisted**, or **Private**.

7. Tap **NEXT**, then let YouTube know whether the video content is kid-friendly.

8. When you're ready, tap **UPLOAD VIDEO**, and the video will be sent to YouTube in the background.

9. To find your uploaded video, tap **Library**, then choose **Your Videos**.

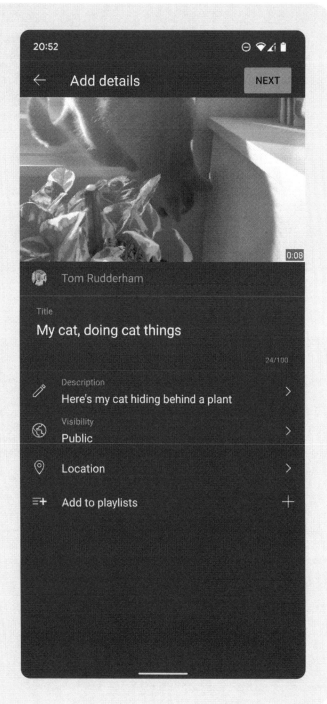

# Share a video

If you would like to send a video to someone else, open it in the YouTube app, then tap the **Share** button. You will then see the following options:

- **Copy link**: This will copy the URL for the video to your phone. You can then open a message, email, note, or document and paste the URL.
- **Gmail**: This will compose a new email with the video's address in the message content.
- **Bluetooth**: Send the video URL to another device over Bluetooth.
- **Message**: Send the video to someone via text message.
- **Keep notes**: Will add the video URL to a new note.
- **Translate**: Your phone will attempt (likely unsuccessfully) to translate the video URL.
- **Nearby Share**: Enables you to send the video to someone else nearby who also has an Android device.

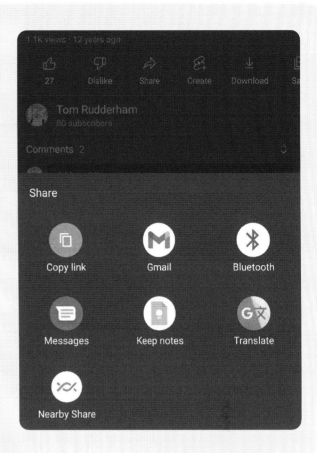

# Explore YouTube's settings

The YouTube app is packed with helpful and interesting settings. You can find them by tapping on your **profile photo** in the top corner, then **Settings**. Here are a few interesting options:

- **Auto-play**. Tell YouTube to not automatically play a new video after the current one has ended.

- **Remind me to take a break**. You'll find this in the General section. It will remind you to do something else after you've spent a considerable amount of time watching YouTube videos.

- **Restricted Mode**. Also under the General section. Once activated, the app will attempt to block videos, including mature content.

- **Captions**. Tap on this setting to customise the size and style of subtitles.

# Get the latest News

## View the latest headlines and featured articles...

With the News app on Android, you'll find all the latest news stories and featured articles in one place. That's because the News app automatically collects all the stories and topics you're interested in then presents them together. It also combines the rich design language typically found in traditional print, along with the interactivity of the web, to create an immersive experience where the story comes to life like never before.

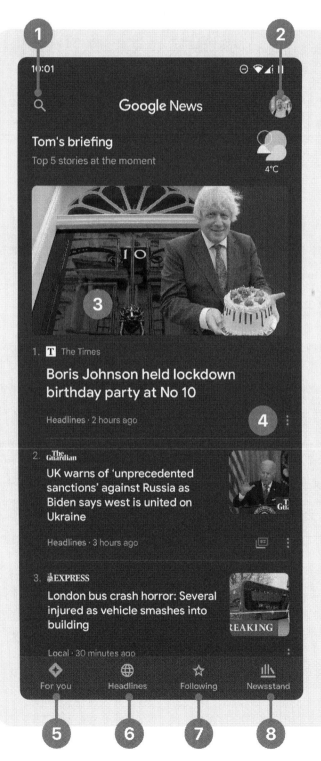

## The basics

1. Quickly find a news topic, source, or location by tapping the **search** button.

2. Tap on your **profile photo** to access notification settings, see your reading history, toggle dark mode, and enable mini cards, which shrink news stories down to three lines maximum.

3. Tap on a news story headline to read the full story.

4. Tap the **options** button below a story to save it for later, share it, or visit the website for the news source.

5. Jump back to the page at any time by tapping this button.

6. See the latest headlines for your location, country, world, or topics.

7. If you're following any news sources (see across the page for more on this), then you can jump straight to them from here.

8. Explore both free and paid-for news sources by tapping Newsstand.

# Follow news sources

To make the most of the News app, you need to tell it what news source or subject matter you'd like to read about. To do this, tap the **Following** button at the bottom of the screen, choose between topic, source, or location, then use the search field to find a news source. When you've found it, tap the **star** icon to start following it.

# Remove news sources

To stop following a news source, tap the **Following** button at the bottom of the screen, choose **View all and manage**, then tap the **options** button to the right of the source that you would like to stop following. Next, use the panel at the bottom of the screen to select **Stop following this topic**.

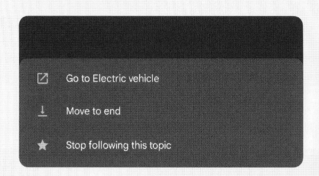

# Save a story for later

While reading a story, tap the **bookmark** icon at the bottom of the screen to save it for later reading. When you're ready to continue reading story, tap **Following**, then scroll down and look for the **Saved Stories** section.

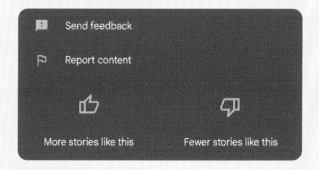

# Suggest similar stories

If you find a news story particularly compelling, then you can tell the News app to recommend more stories like it in the future. To do this, go to the topic where the news story is shown, then tap the **options** button to its right. Next, choose **More stories like this**.

# Use Maps to explore the world

## Discover new places, get route guidance, and more...

With a map of the entire globe in your pocket, it's no longer possible to get lost in a busy city or strange new land. That's exactly what the Maps app gives you, alongside directions, real-time traffic information, transit timetables, 3D views of major cities and more. All of this for free, and fully accessible at any time.

To find the Map app, just unlock your phone and tap on this icon:

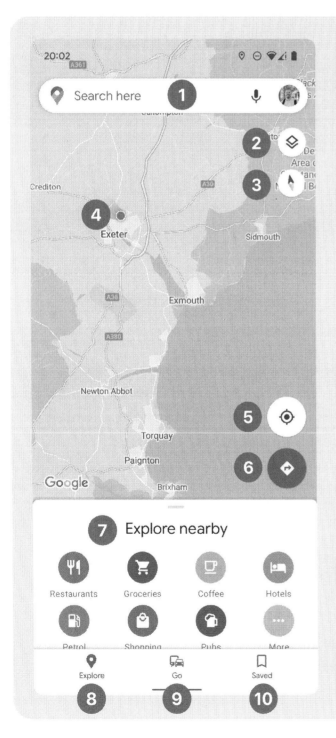

## The basics

**1** Tap on the **search field** to search for a place, address, or landmark.

**2** Tap the **Layers** button to swap view modes (see across page for more).

**3** Tap the **compass arrow** button to reorientate the map north. Tap it for a second time, and the map will rotate to match the orientation of your phone.

**4** This blue dot represents your current location in the world.

**5** Tap this button to jump to your current location.

**6** Tap the **Directions** button to quickly find a route from A to B.

**7** This is the information panel. You can slide it upwards to explore locations in your ares, or get suggestions for places to visit.

**8** Tap the **Explore** button to return to this screen.

**9** Tap **Go** to get directions to your frequently visited places.

**10** Tap **Saved** to access your saved locations list, places you want to go, and starred places.

# Swap view modes

When you open the Maps app, you'll see the world in a colourful vector mode that makes finding locations and landmarks easy. If you'd rather view the world using satallite imagery, see public transport details, or use the driving view, tap the **layers** button in the top right corner, then make a choice using the six options.

# Save a location

If you regularly travel to a location, such as work or home, then it's a good idea to save it. By doing this, you can get directions in an instant by tapping the **Saved** button at the bottom of the screen.

To save a location, either tap on a place or search for it, then tap the **Save** button in the information panel. You can then choose to add the location to your favourites list, places you want to go, or starred locations.

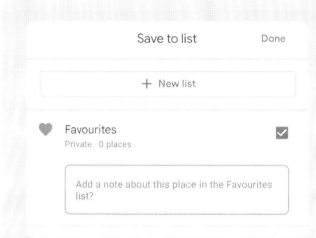

# Explore what's nearby

To find local business and places of interest, tap on the **information panel** field at the bottom of the screen, then use the various icons to see what's nearby. Scroll down, and you'll also find articles and guides to nearby cities.

# Call a business or place of interest

If you're exploring the map and find a local business or place of interest, tap on it to find out more. You might see TripAdvisor reviews, photos, opening times, phone numbers, and useful pieces of information.

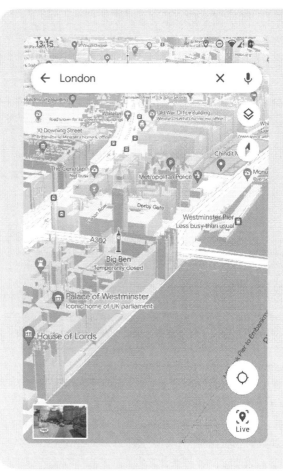

# See a 3D map

Using the Maps app it's possible to navigate the world's most famous cities in beautiful 3D graphics. To view the 3D map, zoom in on the map as close as you can get, tap the **map view** button in the upper-right corner, then choose **3D**. The Maps view will then load a 3D landscape with detailed 3D buildings.

To rotate the image, simply place two fingers on the screen then rotate them. To tilt the camera, simultaneously move two fingers up or down the screen. Moving them left or right will pan the camera.

# Look Around in Street View

Street View lets you explore the world at street level using 360-degree imagery. It's almost like you're walking down the street itself, and it offers an incredible way to explore the cities of the world.

To use Street View mode, zoom the map until you see a thumbnail image of the street appear in the lower-left corner. Once you see it, tap the icon and Street View mode will begin.

To pan the view, just push it with your finger. To move in any direction, double-tap where you want to go. You can also tap on a tag to see more information about a place or business.

One last tip: if you want to use Split Street View mode (see example to the right), where the top half of the screen shows Street View and the bottom half shows the map, **tap and hold** on the map where you want to look, then tap the **Street View** thumbnail in the lower-left corner.

# See live traffic

If you're planning to drive somewhere, then it's often a good idea to see the traffic ahead. Google Maps can show you live traffic conditions as coloured lines on the map. Green indicates smoothly-flowing traffic, orange slow traffic, red very slow traffic, and dark red as almost standstill traffic.

If you don't see these coloured lines on the map, tap the **map view** button in the upper right corner, then tap **Traffic**.

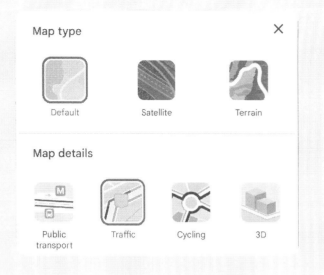

# Search indoor maps

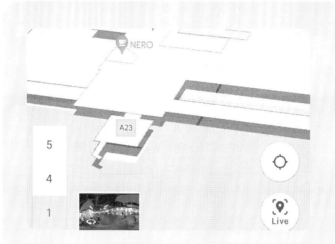

With the Maps app you can find your way around airports and shopping centres using the indoor maps feature, which displays the locations of stores, rest rooms, and more. Most international airports and major shopping malls are fully mapped. To see all of this detail, simply zoom in on a location until you see its interior appear. If there are multiple floors then you'll see buttons to jump between each in the lower left.

# See Transit information

If you're exploring a location using public transport then it's a good idea to view the local area using the Transit view in Maps. This lets you see nearby train stations, tube lines, bus stations, taxi pick-up points and more.

To enable this view simply tap the **map view** button in the upper-right corner of the screen then choose **Public Transport**.

# Search Maps using Google Assistant

If you'd rather search for a place or person using Google Assistant, hold down the **Power** button until Google Assistant appears, then say something like *"where is the nearest hotel?"*

# Turn-by-turn navigation

Satellite navigation and GPS technology have made driving to unfamiliar locations so much easier. With an Android phone, you can take advantage of this same technology to explore and navigate the world. It's wonderfully easy to use. Maps will display the route in 3D, with road signs, written directions, and spoken directions. And if the traffic conditions change, the app will offer an alternative route for you to take.

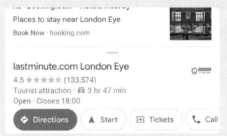

**1** To get started, open Maps then tap the **Search** field in the information panel. Next, enter the destination you wish the navigate to. This can be an address, zip code, or you can tap and hold on the map to drop a pin.

**2** Once you've searched for an address, tap the blue **Directions** button to enable turn-by-turn instructions. Maps will automatically find the optimal route to the destination. It will also offer alternative routes, if any are available, which appear as opaque blue lines on the map. You can tap on these alternative routes to choose them.

**3** Once you've found a suitable route tap the green **GO** button to begin following turn-by-turn directions. Maps will automatically speak directions out-loud when you approach turns, lane changes, and exits - just as you'd expect if using a dedicated Sat-Nav device. You can even press the **Power** button to turn off your phone's display and it will light up whenever a change in direction is needed.

Vauxhall Bridge Millbank (Stop X)

# Drop a pin to learn more

To see detailed information about a specific point, simply **tap and hold** your finger on the screen and a pin will be dropped underneath it. Tap on that pin and you'll see more information about the location, including its address and distance.

# Set custom preferences

You can customise the Maps app to avoid tolls and motorways, show speed limits, and much more. To explore these settings, tap on your **profile photo** in the search bar at the top of the screen, scroll down, then tap **Settings**.

# Get walking or cycling directions

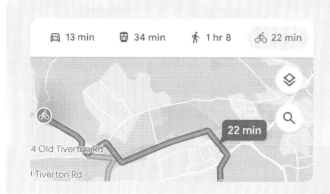

If you're planning a route on foot or a bike, then use the small graphical buttons to select either walking or cycling directions. If going by bike, then you can plan a route that avoids hills and busy roads.

# Suggest an edit

To report an error or missing place, or to suggest an edit, tap on a location or place, expand the information panel at the bottom of the screen, then tap **Suggest an edit**. In the pop-up window you can suggest a change of name or details, mark it as closed, or even non-existent.

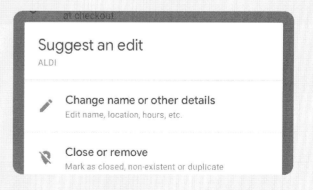

# Notes and Reminders

Learn how to quickly jot down notes, plus much more...

On first glance, the Keep Notes app is a fairly basic way to jot down ideas and lists. It's much more than that, however. With the Keep Notes app you can collaborate with friends, draw and annotate, scan documents, format text, create tables, and more.

## The basics

**1** Return to the overview screen (turn over page, for more on this).

**2** Pin a note to the top of the overview screen.

**3** Remind yourself about a note at a predetermined time or place.

**4** Archive a note.

**5** Tap the **plus (+)** button to insert a photo, drawing, or audio recording.

**6** Customise the look of a note by changing the background colour, or by adding a background graphic.

**7** Undo or redo a change made to a note.

**8** Tap the **options** button to delete a note, copy it, share it with someone else, collaborate on it with another person, or add a label.

# Create a new note

To create a new Note, open the **Keep Notes** app, then tap the **New Note** button in the bottom-right corner. A blank note will then slide into view, and you can begin typing straight away.

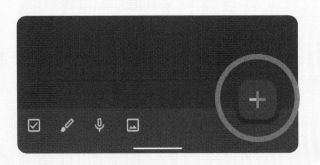

# Sketch in a note

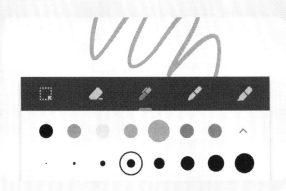

If you'd like to sketch a note, open the **Keep Notes** app, then tap the **pencil** button at the bottom of the screen. A sketchpad will now appear, enabling you to draw with a pen, felt tip or pencil. You can adjust the colour and thickness of the pen by double-tapping the panel at the bottom of the screen.

# Add check box lists

If you're making a list of items (such as a shopping list), then you can create check box lists and then check them off one by one.  To do this, write the first item on the list, tap the **plus (+)** button above the keyboard, then choose **Tick boxes**.

To add a second item press the **return** key. To mark items as complete, tap the **checkbox** to the left of the item.

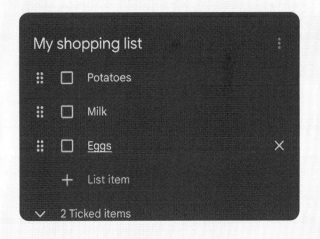

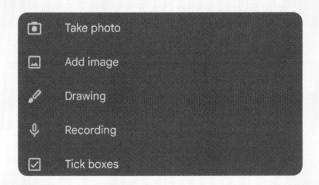

# Insert a photo

While composing a note, tap the **plus (+)** button above the keyboard, then choose **Add image**. You can then either take a photo on the spot, or add a photo from your phone's library. Photos are attached at the top of the note, and you can add as many as you like.

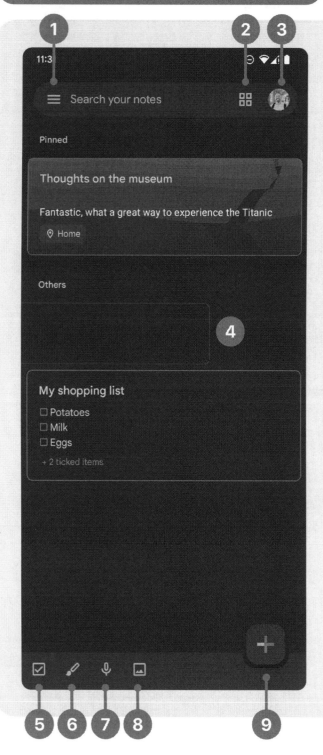

# The Keep Notes overview screen

With multiple notes saved on your phone, an overview screen will appear whenever you open the app. Here's a quick overview of how it works:

**1** Quickly jump between your notes, reminders, labels, archived content, deleted content, or access settings.

**2** Tap this button to toggle between grid and list view.

**3** Tap on your **profile photo** to manage your Google account.

**4** Swipe a note from right to left to archive it.

**5** Create a note containing checklists.

**6** Create a note containing a sketch.

**7** Create an audio recording and save it as a note.

**8** Add a photo straight into a note.

**9** Tap this button to create a new blank note.

# Pin a note

While viewing a note, tap the **pin** button in the top corner. The note will then be pinned at the top of the overview screen, making it easier to find.

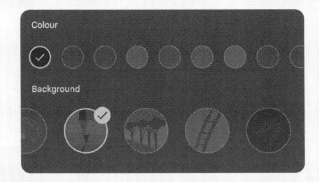

# Customise the look of a note

While editing a note, tap the **colour palette** button at the bottom of the screen. A small pop-up panel will appear, enabling you to change the background colour or assign a pre-made background image.

# Delete a note

While editing a note, tap the **options** button in the bottom right corner, then choose **Delete**. From the overview screen you can swipe a note right to left to delete it.

If you accidentally delete a note then don't worry, you'll have a few seconds after deleting it to tap **Undo**. Alternatively, you can return to the overview screen, tap the **menu** button in the very top left corner, then **Deleted**. On the following screen **tap and hold** on the note you wish to restore, then tap the **restore** button in the upper right corner.

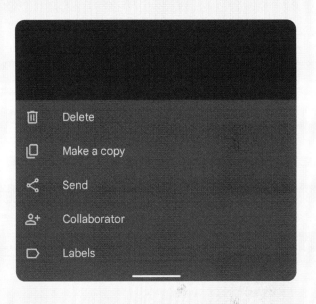

# Dictate a note

Sometimes it's quicker to say what you want, rather than type it key-by-key. To quickly dictate a note:
- From the overview screen tap the **microphone** button.
- If you're already editing a note, tap the **plus (+)** button, then choose **Recording**.

Your phone will start listening to you. Simply say out loud what you would like to include in the note. You can use punctuation too, by saying "*full stop*", "*comma*", or "*explanation mark*".

Leave a pause when you've finished dictating, and the app will automatically enter your spoken words as text. It will also include a recording of your voice. You can hear this back by tapping the **play** button, or delete it by tapping the **trash** button.

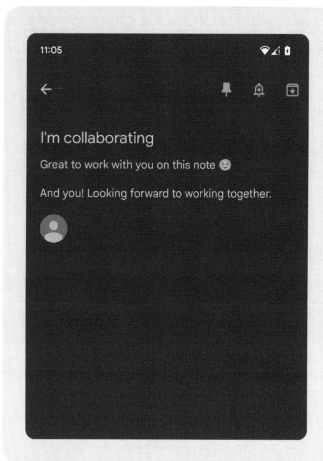

# Collaborate on a note

To share a note with someone else, tap the **options** button in the bottom right corner, then choose **Collaborator**. Next, enter the name or email address of the person you would like to share the note with. You can add multiple people by entering a comma after the name or address.

When you share a note, you can do the following:
- View, edit and delete the note.
- See, add and delete other people.
- Stop sharing the note.
- Delete the note.

People you have shared a note with can:
- View and edit the note.
- See who else is sharing the list.

To stop sharing a note, tap on the **profile photo** of the person within the note, then tap the **X** button next to their name or email address.

# Create a new Reminder

Sometimes it's a good idea to set a reminder for later in the day, another day, or even when you arrive at a location.

To start a new reminder, create a new note and give it a title. Make sure the title is something that will make sense when the time comes for the reminder to activate. Next, tap the **bell** icon at the top of the screen. You'll see a large number of options appear, which we will explain over the next two pages...

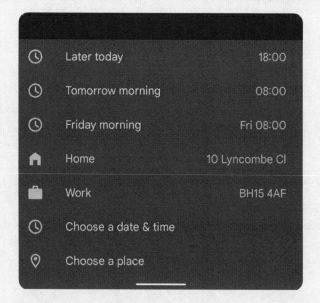

# Set a reminder for a later in the day

To set a reminder for later in the day, tap on **Later today**. By default, it will be set to 18:00, but you can change this by tapping on **Today, 18:00**, then using the options to pick an exact time.

Note! Make sure Do Not Disturb is deactivated, otherwise you won't receive the reminder notification.

# Set a location reminder

Similarly, you can also remind yourself when you reach a location. To do this, tap the **bell** icon to create a reminder and then select **Choose a place** in the pop-up window. You can then choose from your home, place of work, or a specific location. If you choose the latter, then you can enter an address or zip/post code.

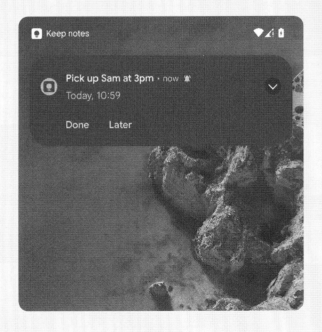

# Mark a reminder as complete

When a reminder is due, your phone will let you know in two ways:

1. If your phone is locked, you'll hear a "ping" and see a notification on the Lock Screen.

2. If you're using the phone, you'll see a notification appear at the top of the screen.

To dismiss this reminder, tap the **Done** button. If you'd like to be re-reminded at a later time, tap **Later** and then choose a time or date.

# Use Google Pay to buy things

## Quickly make purchases with your phone...

Google Pay is a fast, simple way to pay for things with your phone. You can use Google Pay at contactless readers within stores, when using apps, or when purchasing things online. There is no maximum transaction limit when you use your phone and card. Your payment info is also protected with multiple layers of security so you can pay with peace of mind – all the time.

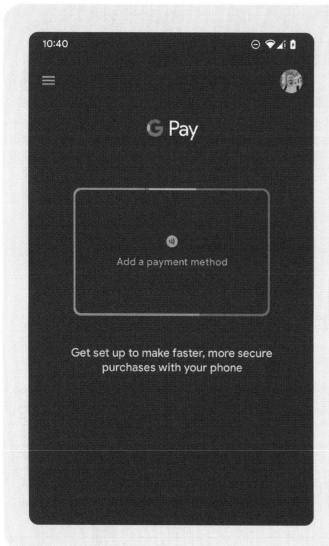

## Set up Google Pay

Before you get started, make sure you have a debit or credit card to hand, as Google Pay won't work without one. Once you're ready...

1. Open the **Google Pay** app. If you've never used it before, tap **GET STARTED**.

2. Tap **Add a payment** method.

3. Choose a card from your Google account, or tap **Credit or debit card**.

4. Use the camera view to point your phone at your credit or debit card. Make sure it's the side with the long set of numbers on. Your phone will automatically recognise the numbers and input them.

5. Enter any details that were not automatically entered, such as the CVC number, then tap **Save**.

6. Google will talk to your bank and display any terms and conditions. After these have been accepted and your details have been verified, your card will be ready to use.

## It's not just debit and credit cards you can add to Google Pay

You can also add loyalty and gift cards, and even public transport passes. To do this open the Google Pay app, then tap **Add a card**. In the pop-up panel you can choose between Loyalty, Gift cards, and public transport.

# Pay for something in a store

When you're ready to pay for something in a store, wake your phone by tapping on the screen or by pressing the **power** button, then tap the cards button in the bottom right corner.

Next, select the card you wish to use, then confirm your ID by using your fingerprint or passcode. You can then hold your phone near the contactless reader to make the payment.

# Pay in an app or online

When you shop online or in apps like Uber and Airbnb, you can pay faster by using Google Pay, rather than manually entering your card details. Keep in mind that you can only do this when you see the Google Pay logo at the checkout.

If you're shopping and see the Google Pay logo, simply tap on it, choose a card, then confirm your order.

# See recent transactions

You can see a list of transactions that you made using Google Pay, download monthly statements, and manage transaction notifications on your phone. To do this, tap the **menu** button in the top left corner, then choose **Activity**.

## Remove a card

If you no longer wish to use a card, open the **Google Pay** app, tap on the card you'd like to remove, then tap the **options** button in the top right corner. Next, choose **Remove payment method**, then confirm via the pop-up window.

# Manage your files

## Free up space, manage files, and be in control...

The Files app on your Android phone is a helpful file management tool that helps you free up space, find files on your device, share files offline with others, and back up files to the cloud. By using the Files app to clear out unwanted files, you can keep your phone running smoothly and ensure that it's always possible to download more content.

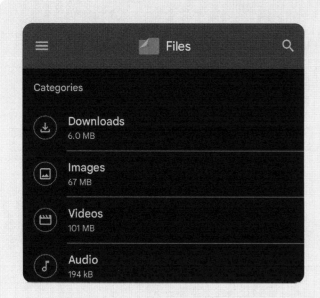

## Explore the Files on your phone

The Files app breaks down all of the things on your phone into various categories, including downloads, images, videos, audio, documents, and apps. To explore each one in detail, open the Files app then tap **Browse**. You'll then see these categories running down the screen, with a breakdown of how much storage each is taking up.

## Clear up space

If you're running out of space to take more photos or install more apps, then the Files app can suggest things to clear out, such as temporary files, unused apps, and old photos that have been backed up to Google Photos. With a tap of your finger, it can then clear these away, leaving you with more space to do important things.

To tidy up your phone and get back some storage space, open the Files app and tap **Clean**. The Files app will then show any suggestions it has found for tidying up your phone. Use these suggestions as you see fit to make more space available.

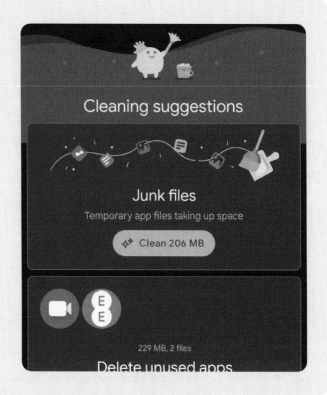

# Search for files

If you're looking for a specific file, open the Files app, tap **Browse**, then tap the **search** button in the top right corner. You can then use the keyboard to search for files, photos, and documents stored on your phone.

# Share a file

To send a file, photo, or document to someone else, tap the **options** button to its right, then choose **Share**. In the pop-up panel, you'll see a number of options, including sending a file via the Messages app, Gmail, or Google Drive.

Perhaps the most helpful method of sharing a file is via **Nearby**. This lets you send a file to another Android user within close proximity. It works directly from one device to another, without using mobile data or connecting to Wi-Fi. Tap this option, wait for the other person to appear, then tap **Send**.

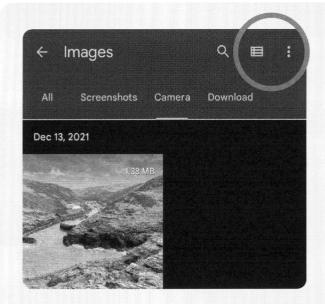

# Sort and display files

The Files app is surprisingly flexible, enabling you to sort files by date, size, and name. You can also swap between grid and list views.

To access these views, tap **Browse** and choose a category, such as Images.

To sort files, tap the **options** button in the top right corner, tap **Sort by**, then make a choice.

To toggle between grid and list views, tap the **view** button in the upper right corner.

# Translate languages

## Talk or type to someone in another language...

If you're planning a trip abroad, need to translate a menu or sign, or want to talk to someone else in another language, then the Google Translate app is an incredibly useful tool. It can translate text, handwriting, photos and speech in over 100 languages, making international conversations much more efficient than talking slowly, loudly, and while making desperate hand gestures.

## The basics

Open the Google Translate app and you'll see a simple screen with a large space for entering text. Here's how it works:

**1** Tap the **star** button to access any saved transcripts and phrases.

**2** Tap on your **profile photo** to access saved transcripts, see your translated history, download additional languages, and access common settings.

**3** Tap here to type a word or phrase that you would like to translate.

**4** Tap on these two buttons to toggle between more than 100 languages.

**5** Tap **Conversation** to (you guessed it), talk to someone in real-time. See across the page for more on this.

**6** Tap the **microphone** button to instantly translate your voice to another language.

**7** Tap **Camera** to take a photo of text in another language and translate it to another.

# Type text

If you want to quickly translate a phrase or word, then tap **Enter text** and type something. As you write, you'll see the translation appear above the keyboard.

Once you've finished typing, press the **enter** button on the keyboard and the Translate app will offer buttons to copy the translation, hear it spoken out-loud, or show you a detailed definition.

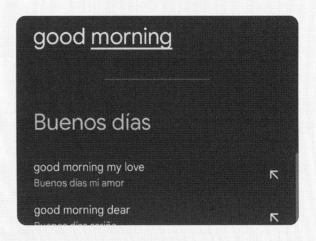

# Have a conversion with someone

The most natural way to communicate with someone is to talk out loud. The Google Translate app lets you do this and will attempt to translate your words in real-time. Here's how it works:

1. Open the **Translate** app, then tap the **Conversation** button.

2. Tap the **Auto** button at the bottom of the screen. This will tell the app to automatically recognise the language being spoken.

3. Speak out loud, and watch as the translation appears as text on the screen. The app will also speak the translation out loud. Continue with your conversation, leaving a pause for the app to translate each sentence.

# Translate text with the Camera

If you'd like to translate something in the real world, such as a photo, menu, or sign, then you can let the Translate app do all the work.

To do this, open the **Translate** app, then tap the **Camera** button in the bottom right corner. Next, point your phone at the text you wish to translate. After a moment, you'll see it instantly translate. It works best if there are small amounts of clear, eligible text.

# Set a timer, alarm, or stopwatch

### Ensure you go to bed at a timely manner, or quickly set a timer...

With the Clock app, it's possible to take control of your day by setting alarms, timers, and even reminding yourself when to go to bed. You'll find the Clock app already installed on your phone. To find it swipe upwards from the Home screen or tap the **All apps** button.

## Remind yourself to go to bed

Using the Clock app, you can choose a regular bedtime, disconnect from your phone, and listen to soothing sounds. To do this:

1. Open the **Clock** app, then tap **Bedtime**.

2. Tap **Get Started**, then choose the time you'd like to wake up.

3. To specify days (such as weekdays), un-tap the days that you don't need a bedtime reminder.

4. You can gently wake yourself up by slowly brightening the screen before the alarm triggers.

5. Tap **Next**, then assign a time you'd like to go to bed. Usually, 8 hours before you get up is a good time.

6. Tap **Next**, and you'll see an overview of your bedtime schedule.

7. If you would like to listen to soothing sounds before you fall asleep, tap **Choose a sound**. You can then choose between free sounds or sound effects from Spotify, YouTube, or Calm.

8. To configure or delete a bedtime schedule, open the **Clock** app, tap **Bedtime**, then tap on a schedule to edit it.

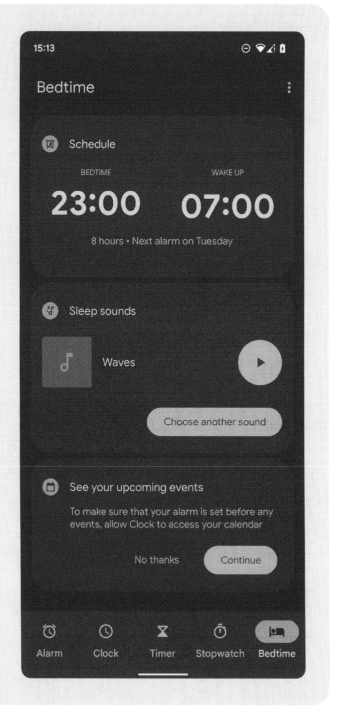

# Set an alarm

If you'd like to set a separate alarm to your bedtime reminder, then open the **Clock** app, tap **Alarm**, then tap the large **plus (+)** button at the bottom of the screen. Next, drag the small control around the clock to choose a time. If you'd rather type an exact time, tap the **keyboard** button then enter a specific time.

Tap **OK** when you've chosen a time for your alarm. You can then assign a schedule by tapping the letters for each day of the week.

# See the local time for another location

Using the Clock app you can see the local time for any number of locations around the world. To do this, open the **Clock** app, tap **Clock**, then tap the large **plus (+)** button at the bottom of the screen. Next, search for a city or location, and select it from the list. It will then be added to the Clock app for you to check whenever needed.

# Set a timer

Open the **Clock** app, select **Timer**, then tap on the **wheel** to start a two-minute timer. To assign a specific length, tap the **plus (+)** button, then enter a length of time using the keypad. When you're ready to start the timer, press the **play** button.

# Use a stopwatch

Open the **Clock** app, select **Stopwatch**, then tap on the **play** button to start a timer. Tap the **stopwatch** button in the lower right corner to set a lap, or tap the **reset** button over on the left to clear the stopwatch.

# Personal Safety

## Keep your health and personal details up to date...

The Personal Safety app is a helpful tool for ensuring you receive help when it's most needed. It can automatically call the emergency services, share your real-time location and critical info with your emergency contacts, notify you about natural disasters and public emergencies, and even detect when you've been in a car crash.

The Personal Safety app is built into every Pixel phone. If you have a phone made by another manufacturer, such as Samsung, then you can download the app for free from the Google Play Store.

## Set up Personal Safety

Open the Personal Safety app for the first time and you'll be welcomed by the set up screen. Here are the steps you need to take to get it up and working:

1. Open the **Personal Safety** app, then tap **Continue as [your name]**.

2. The first step is to add an emergency contact. Their details will be available on your phone's lock screen in an emergency, so make sure it's someone that you can trust. Tap **+ Add contact**, choose someone from your contacts book, then tap **Next**.

3. Add your medical information, including blood type and allergies. Tap **More** to add additional information such as medications, address, and medical notes, then **Done** to finish setting up the Personal Safety app.

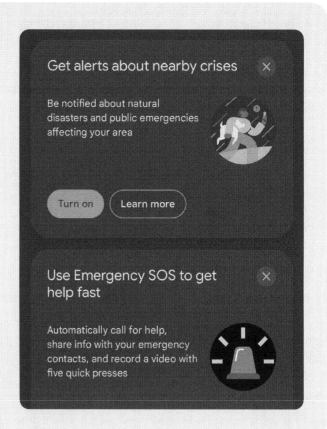

## Toggle features on

With the Personal Safety app set up, you can now start activating its many features. To do this scroll through the features available, and tap **Turn on** to activate each.

You can also tap the **menu** button in the top left corner to access all of the Personal Safety features and settings.

# Emergency SOS

If you find yourself in an emergency, then your phone call automatically call the emergency services, share your information with emergency contacts, and even record a video.

To set up Emergency SOS mode, open the **Personal Safety** app, look for the **Emergency SOS** panel, then tap on it. Next, follow the on-screen instructions to toggle this feature on.

To activate Emergency SOS mode, press the **Power** button quickly five times. A five-second timer will appear on-screen, followed by a very loud chime. To cancel Emergency SOS mode, use the **slider** at the bottom of the screen.

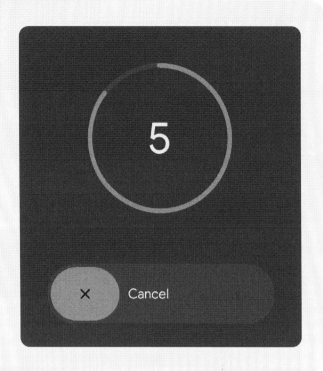

# Emergency sharing

In an emergency, your real-time location and information can be shared with others, including when you start and end an emergency call, whether your battery is low, and your current location.

To turn all of these features on, open the **Personal Safety** app, look for the **Emergency sharing** panel, then tap on it. Next, follow the on-screen instructions to toggle this feature on.

With Emergency sharing now set up, you can activate it at any time by opening the **Personal Safety** app, then tapping the large red **Emergency sharing** button at the bottom of the screen.

# An overview of the Settings app

## Get to know the basics of Settings...

Whenever you want to make a change to your phone, adjust a setting, or update the operating system, then the Settings app is the place to go.

You can easily find the Settings app by looking for the icon with a cog gear in its centre:

Open the Settings app and you'll see a list of shortcuts to all the important settings on your phone. They're labelled logically, so if you want to adjust how apps notify you, then tap on Notifications. Similarly, if you want to connect to a new Wi-Fi network, tap Network and Internet.

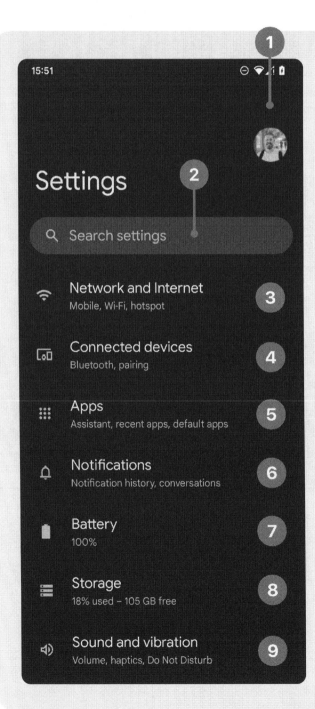

## The basics

We'll explore all of the important settings you need to know about over the next few pages. In the meantime, here's a quick overview of the Settings app:

**1** Tap on your **profile photo** to manage your Google account, see your device details, your phone number, adjust emergency information, and manage your Google Pay cards.

**2** Quickly find a specific setting by searching for it.

**3** Toggle WiFi, VPN, enable Aeroplane mode and turn your phone into a hotspot.

**4** Manage any devices connected to your phone.

**5** See recently opened apps, assign default apps, adjust Google Assistant, and see how long you've spent using your phone.

**6** Toggle a variety of notification settings from here.

**7** See the current battery life, toggle Battery Saver mode, and see which apps have been using the most battery power.

**8** See which apps and content are using up space on your phone, and free up space by offloading unused files.

**9** Adjust volumes, assign new ringtones, and customise the sound effects your phone makes.

# Search through Settings

The Settings app is packed with toggle switches, fields, and features for customising how your phone works. Many are hidden away in sub-sections that you probably wouldn't find unless you were really determined, so if you need to quickly change a setting, open the **Settings** app and tap on the **search bar** at the top of the screen. You can now look for something specific by entering just a few letters.

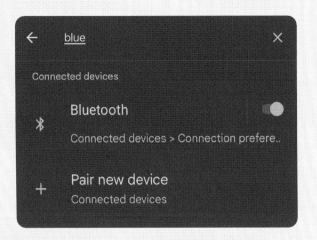

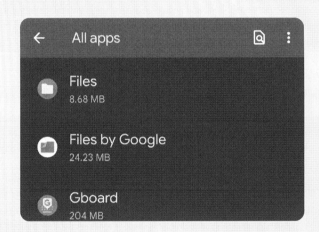

# Find individual app settings

To access individual app settings, open **Settings** and tap **Apps**. Next, tap **> See all apps** and you'll see a list of every app on your phone. Select one, then use the shortcuts to jump to a specific setting.

# Device information

Tap on your **profile photo** in the top right corner, then tap on **Device**, and you'll see a wealth of information about your phone, including:

- **Device name**. Tap on this to rename your phone.
- **Google Account**. Sync your Google account or sign out.
- **Phone number**. Helpful if you've forgotten it.
- **Model**. The exact model of your phone.
- **IMEI**. Think of this as the serial number for your device.
- **Android version**. See what version of Android you're running. At the time of writing the latest version is 12.

# Adjust volume settings

Open the **Settings** app and choose **Sounds & vibration**, and you'll see a large range of audio options appear. The sliders near the top of the screen enable you to alter the volume levels of media, calls, ringtones and alarms, while toggle buttons at the bottom let you turn off lock sounds, touch sounds, and dial pad tones.

# Change a text or ringtone alert

From the same **Sounds & vibration** panel, notice the **Phone ringtone** shortcut below the sliders. Tap this to choose from a wide variety of ringtone alerts. Choose an option (such as **Pixel Sounds**), then tap on a sound effect to preview and select it.

# Turn off touch feedback

Your phone will automatically vibrate every time you press a key on the on-screen keyboard. If you find this distracting, then it's possible to turn this feature off. To do this, open the **Sounds & vibration** panel, tap **Vibration and haptics**, then lower the **Touch feedback** slider.

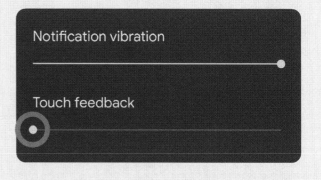

# Turn off System Haptics

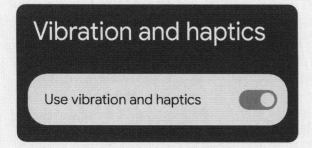

Every now and then your phone will make a subtle vibration to let you know something has happened. To disable these vibrations, go to the **Sounds & vibration** panel, tap **Vibration and haptics**, then toggle **Use vibration and haptics** off.

# Prevent an app from tracking your location

Many apps will track your location as you go from place to place. Often this can be helpful, such as when you're using the Maps app to find your way around; but other apps, such as Facebook, might use your location to offer personalised adverts.

To prevent an app from tracking your location, open the **Settings** app, scroll down and then tap on **Location**.

If you don't want any apps to know your location, then toggle **Use location** off.

Under **Recent access,** you'll see any apps that have recently tracked your location. Tap on an app to adjust or remove its ability to track you.

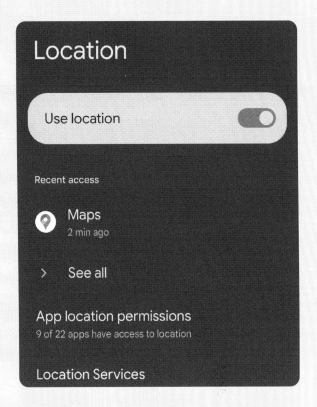

# Hotspot tethering

With hotspot tethering, you can share your phone's 4G or 5G signal with other devices over Wi-Fi. This can be particularly helpful if you're away from home with lots of electronic devices (such as laptops, gaming consoles, or even other phones), as they can all be connected to your phone to share its wireless connection. To turn on hotspot tethering:

1. Open the **Settings** app, tap **Network and Internet**, then tap **Hotspot and tethering**.

2. Tap **Wi-Fi hotspot**, then toggle **Wi-Fi hotspot** on.

3. Tap on **Hotspot name** and change it to something recognisable.

4. Tap on **Hotspot password**. This will reveal the password other devices will need to enter to use your phone's connection. You can change this if needed.

5. Your hotspot is now ready. Using another device, open its Wi-Fi settings, select your phone's hotspot, then enter the correct password. With a little luck you'll be instantly connected and able to use the web.

# Display settings

## Toggle dark and light modes, the lock timer, and more...

The display of your phone is its most crucial component, because it's the one you spend the most time prodding, poking, and stroking. The Android operating system enables you to heavily customise how the display works, from how long it takes for the screen to turn off, to how smoothly content scrolls, to how large the text is.

## Screen timeout

Each Android phone will automatically turn off the display and lock the device after a certain amount of time. Typically this is five minutes, but if you would like to save some battery power, and also reduce the risk of someone using your phone while it's unlocked, then it's a good idea to change how long it takes for the screen to turn off. To do this:

**1** Open the **Settings** app, tap **Display**, then tap **Screen timeout**.

**2** Choose a desired amount of time. Options include 15 seconds, 1 minute, and 30 minutes.

### Screen timeout

- ○ 15 seconds
- ○ 30 seconds
- ◉ 1 minute
- ○ 2 minutes
- ○ 5 minutes

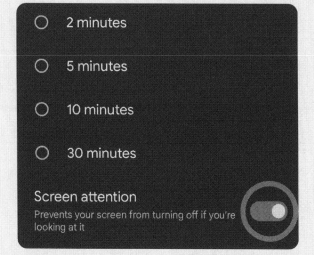

## Use Screen attention

If you have one of the latest Android phones, then you might be able to use a clever feature called Screen attention. It works by using the front camera to see if you are looking at the screen. If so, the screen will stay on until you look away, then it will automatically lock itself after the Screen timeout setting has been met.

To turn on Screen attention, open the **Settings** app, tap **Display**, then tap **Screen timeout**. Next, scroll down and toggle **Screen attention** on.

# Turn off Dark theme

By default, many Android phones use the Dark theme for menus and general use. When this is activated, text is coloured white and shown over a dark background.

You can deactivate Dark theme to give your phone a brighter, more cheerful look. To do this, open the **Settings** app, select **Display**, then toggle **Dark theme** off.

Screen timeout
After 5 minutes of inactivity

Appearance

Dark theme
Will never turn on automatically

Font size
Default

# Toggle Adaptive brightness

Your phone will automatically adjust the brightness of the display to match the light levels of the environment around you. This means when you're sitting in a dark room, the screen will lower the brightness, and when you're in direct sunlight, the screen will maximise its brightness.

If you would like to deactivate this feature, then open the **Settings** app, select **Display**, then toggle **Adaptive brightness** off.

# Adjust text size

If you're finding it difficult to read the text on your phone, then it's possible to dramatically increase its size, making everything from app names to text on the web larger. To do this:

1. Open the **Settings** app, tap **Display**, then tap **Font size**.

2. Use the **slider** at the bottom of the screen to decrease or increase the text size on your phone. As you move the slider, you'll see example text above change in real-time.

3. After making a change, close the settings app and you'll see that all text on your phone has changed in size.

Oz

Even with eyes protected by the green spectacles Dorothy and her friends were at first dazzled by the brilliancy of the wonderful City. The streets were lined with beautiful houses all built of green marble and studded everywhere with sparkling emeralds. They walked over a pavement of the same green marble, and where the blocks were joined together were rows of emeralds, set closely, and glittering in the brightness of the sun. The window panes were of green glass; even the sky above the City had a green tint, and the rays of the sun were green.

Preview

Large

A ———————⊙———— A

Make the text on screen smaller or larger.

# Use a screen saver

Think of a screen saver as an interesting way to fill your phone's screen when it is charging or plugged into a dock. There are three screen saver options to choose from: a clock, a set of pulsating colours, or photos stored on your device. To enable the screen saver feature:

1. Open the **Settings** app, tap **Display**, then tap **Screen saver**.

2. Tap **Current screen saver** and choose whether to show a clock, colours, or photos. If you choose photos, tap the **back arrow** then tap the **settings** button to choose a set of photos stored on your phone.

3. Tap **When to start**, and tell your phone to show the screen saver when it is charging, docked, or both.

4. Finally, toggle on **Use screen saver**. You'll see the screen saver immediately take over the screen. You can cancel it at any moment by tapping on the screen.

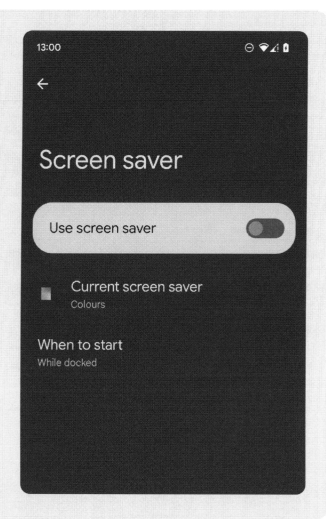

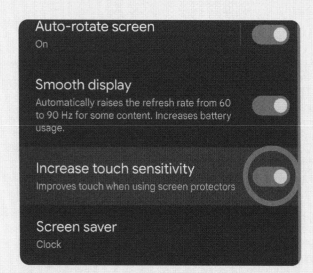

# Increase the touch sensitivity

If you're using a screen protector, then you might find the screen less sensitive to your taps and swipes. To counter this, you can tell your phone to increase its touch sensitivity levels so that it better detects the static from your fingertip. To do this, open the **Settings** app, tap **Display**, then toggle **Increase touch sensitivity** on.

# Use Screen time to set limits

## See how long you've spent on your phone, and set app limits...

If you're concerned or worried that you might be spending too long using your phone, then the Screen time panel included in the Settings app will help you work out exactly how long you've spent using apps, how many notifications you've received, or set time limits to prevent the overuse of apps.

## Find Screen time

1. Open the **Settings** app, select **Apps**, then tap on **Screen time**.

2. You'll see an overview of how long you've spent using your phone over the last week, with the total number of minutes for each day.

3. To see how many notifications you've received, tap the **drop-down** button near the top of the screen called **Screen time**, then choose **Notifications received**.

4. To see how many times you've unlocked your phone over the last week, tap that same **drop-down** button, then choose **Times opened**.

## Limit how long you can spend using an app

If you'd like to limit how long you can spend each day using an app, then the Screen time panel can help:

1. Open the **Settings** app, select **Apps**, then tap on **Screen time**.

2. Scroll down and tap on **Show all [number] of apps**. This will display all the apps on your phone.

3. To set a time limit for a particular app, tap the **timer** button, then use the controls in the pop-up panel. Tap **OK** to save your settings.

Now, if you're using an app and the limit is reached, the app will be paused for the rest of the day.

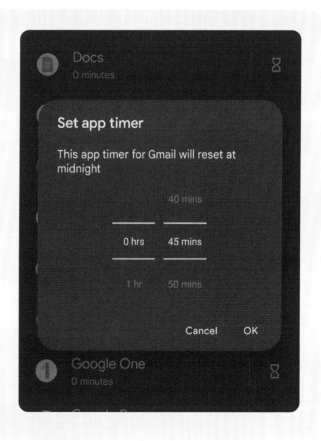

# Security settings

## Check for updates and ensure your device is secure from threats...

Your phone contains incredibly personal information, such as text messages, passwords, photos, and banking details. It's imperative to ensure no one can access this information when your phone is left alone, which is why Google has included a helpful security panel in the Settings app.

## Get a security overview

1. Open the **Settings** app, then select **Security**. You'll see any immediate risks flagged at the top of the screen.

2. If a risk is flagged, tap on it to see more details. For example, you might have saved passwords that are easy to guess, or two-step verification disabled.

3. To explore further settings, scroll down and tap on the various choices. We'll explore the most important ones over this spread of pages.

## Check for harmful apps

Google does a great job and making sure harmful apps are not allowed into the Google Play Store, but if you've stumbled across an app that contains malware, or shares your details on the web, then you can quickly track down these apps and remove them. Here's how:

1. Open the **Settings** app, select **Security**, then tap on **App security**.

2. If any harmful apps are detected, then they will be flagged and you can remove them straight away. If everything is clear and you'd like to double-check, then tap **Scan** and your phone will do another sweep.

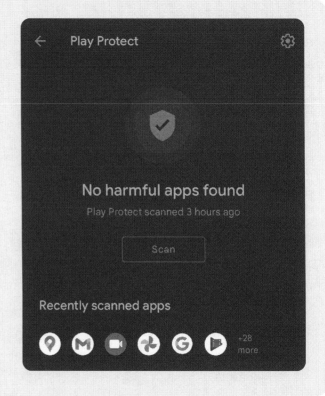

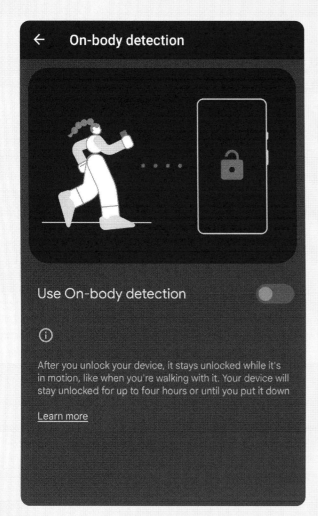

**Use On-body detection**

ⓘ

After you unlock your device, it stays unlocked while it's in motion, like when you're walking with it. Your device will stay unlocked for up to four hours or until you put it down

Learn more

# Activate Smart Lock

Smart Lock works by detecting if your phone is in your pocket or near your home and if so, keep your phone unlocked. It's worth noting that neither is foolproof. Your phone can't tell if it is in someone else's pocket, nor can it tell if it's you or someone else in your home that's looking at the screen. Nevertheless, this is a helpful feature to have. To activate it:

**1** Open the **Settings** app, select **Security**, tap **Advanced settings**, then choose **Smart Lock**. Enter your PIN if asked.

**2** To keep your phone unlocked when it's in your pocket, tap **On-body detection**, then toggle it **on**.

**3** To unlock your phone when you're home, tap **Trusted places**, then tap **+ Add trusted place**. You can then use Google maps to select a location.

**4** You can also keep your phone unlocked when certain devices are connected, such as Bluetooth headphones. To do this, tap **Trusted devices**, then tap **+ Add trusted device**.

# Be warned about suspicious messages

Suspicious messages often include fake links, unusual requests, or attempt to scam you, so it's important to be warned about them. Your phone can alert you when it thinks a suspicious text message has arrived. To turn on this feature:

**1** Open the **Settings** app, select **Security**, tap **Advanced settings**, then choose **Suspicious message alerts**.

**2** Toggle **Show alerts** on. Now, if any suspicious messages are sent to your phone, it will try to warn you.

← 

## Suspicious message alerts

Show alerts ⬤

ⓘ

These alerts let you know if a text message includes a suspicious request, fake link or potential scam. Your phone privately processes and protects message content. Your messages aren't shared with any apps, websites or companies

# Look after your battery

## Learn how to manage your phone's battery and more...

You might not know it, but batteries don't last forever. That's because every time you recharge your phone, a tiny fraction of its battery capacity is lost. This means that if you recharge your device every night, after a year it might lose up to ten percent of its original capacity.

The latest Android phones do a pretty good job at alleviating this problem thanks to some clever battery management techniques, but nevertheless, over time they will degrade to a small extend. Here's how you can see how your battery is faring, and what to do if it has degraded more than you were expecting...

## Take a glance at your battery

To access the battery overview screen, open the **Settings** app, then tap on **Battery**. You'll see the battery's percentage remaining, an estimate of how long the phone will stay powered in lock mode, and various shortcuts to battery-related settings.

## Activate Battery Saver

Battery Saver mode attempts to save battery life by turing on Dark mode, limiting background activity checks, visual effects, and certain network features. To activate it:

1. Open the **Settings** app, select **Battery**, then tap on **Battery Saver**.

2. Toggle **Use Battery Saver** on.

Extreme Battery Saver

Extend your battery life further in critical moments. Extreme Battery Saver pauses most apps and notifications. Select your essential apps so that you don't miss important notifications or messages.

When to use
Never use

# Use Extreme Battery Saver mode

If you're concerned about battery life, then it's possible to extend your battery life in critical moments with a feature called Extreme Battery Saver. It pauses most apps and notifications, turns off Wi-Fi, hotspot mode, and certain features like 'Hey Google'. To activate Extreme Battery Saver:

1. Open the **Settings** app, select **Battery**, then tap on **Battery Saver**.

2. Tap on **Extreme Battery Saver**.

3. Tap **When to use**, then select either **Ask every time**, or **Always use**.

4. If you would like to ensure that certain apps are not affected by Extreme Battery mode, then go back to the Extreme Battery Saver panel and tap **Essential apps**. You can then select which apps can always use all of your phone's resources.

# Schedule Battery Saver

You can ask Battery Saver mode to automatically kick in when the battery reaches a certain percentage, or when your phone thinks you'll need to preserve power. To do this:

1. Open the **Settings** app, select **Battery**, then tap on **Battery Saver**.

2. Tap on **Set a schedule**.

3. If you have a predictable schedule (say, you work the same hours every day and use similar apps around the same time each day), then choose **Based on your routine**, and your phone will guess when to activate Battery Saver mode.

4. If you would rather activate Battery Saver mode when the battery's percentage reaches a certain level, then select **Based on percentage** and make a choice using the slider.

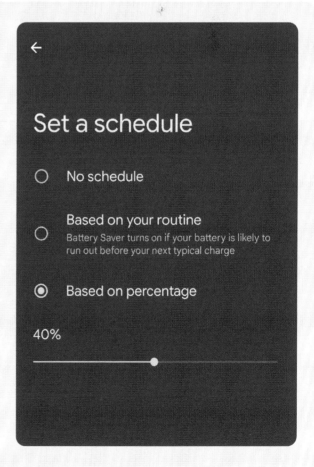

Set a schedule

○ No schedule

○ Based on your routine
Battery Saver turns on if your battery is likely to run out before your next typical charge

◉ Based on percentage

40%

# Digital Wellbeing & Parental Controls

## Discover how much time you've spent using your phone, and limit future distractions...

If you're concerned or worried that you might be spending too long using your phone, then the Digital Wellbeing panel included in the Settings app will help you work out exactly how long you've spent using apps, how many notifications you've received, or set time limits to prevent future distractions.

## Get an overview of how you've used your phone

Open the **Settings** app, then select **Digital Wellbeing and parental controls**. You'll see an overview of how long you've spent using your phone for the day, broken down by apps, unlocks, and notifications.

## Bedtime mode

It's a good idea to wind down at the end of the day by limiting the amount of time you spend on your phone. Bedtime mode attempts to help by changing the screen to black and white, silencing your phone, and letting only important calls come through. To activate Bedtime mode:

1. Open the **Settings** app, select **Digital Wellbeing and parental controls**, then tap on **Bedtime mode**.

2. To set a schedule, tap on the timers, then assign days of the week using the buttons below.

3. To toggle greyscale mode and Do Not Disturb, tap on **Customise**, then make a choice.

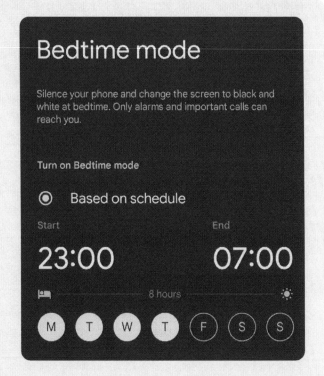

## Flip to Shhh

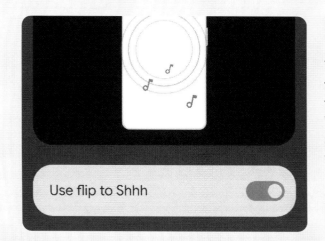

You can instantly turn on Do Not Disturb mode by turning your phone upside down and placing it on a flat surface. To do this, go to **Settings**, select **Digital Wellbeing and parental controls**, then tap **Flip to Shhh**. Next, toggle **Use flip to Shhh** on, then place your phone upside down.

## Set up Parental controls

If you manage the phone of a child, then it's possible to enable content restrictions to prevent them from accessing unsuitable material. You can also set limits and block apps. Here's how it works:

1. Open the **Settings** app, select **Digital Wellbeing and parental controls**, scroll all the way down, then tap on Set up parental controls.

2. On the following screen, tap **Get started**. You can then assign the device to a child, teenager, or adult.

3. Follow the on-screen prompts to link a Google account for the person with your own, choose apps and set limits, and set controls such as bedtime and screen time limits.

## Heads Up

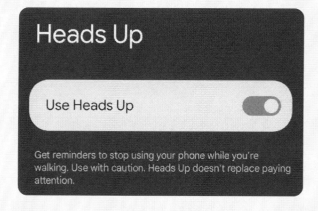

If you're walking while using your phone, you can get a friendly reminder to focus on what's happening around you with a feature called Heads Up. To activate it, go to **Settings** > **Digital Wellbeing and parental controls**, then tap on **Heads Up**. Next, follow the on-screen prompts to allow your phone to know when you're walking, and then you're ready to go.

# Accessibility settings

## Enable visual, audio, and physical accommodations...

Your phone might be an intuitive device to use, but it's also packed with assistive features to help those with visual impairments or motor control limitations. You'll find the majority of them in the Accessibility panel within the Settings app. To get there, open **Settings** then select **Accessibility**.

## Ask your phone to read out-loud with TalkBack

TalkBack is a screen reader intended for situations or people who have difficulty seeing the screen. When activated, the focused item on the screen is spoken out loud.

To turn on TalkBack, go to **Settings > Accessibility > TalkBack**, then toggle **Use TalkBack** on.

**How to use TalkBack**
- Swipe right or left to move between items.
- Double-tap to activate an item.
- Drag two fingers to scroll.

You can toggle TalkBack on or off at any time by holding down both **volume keys** for a few seconds.

### TalkBack

Use TalkBack

---

**Display size**
Default

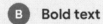
**Bold text**

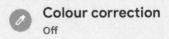
**Colour correction**
Off

## Bold text

By bolding all text on your phone, you can make it easier to read small words and buttons. To do this, go to **Settings > Text & Display**, then toggle **Bold text** on.

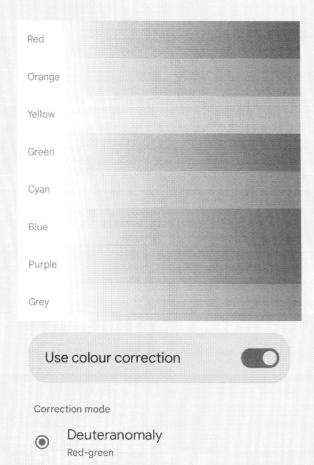

Colour correction

Red

Orange

Yellow

Green

Cyan

Blue

Purple

Grey

Use colour correction

Correction mode

◉ Deuteranomaly
Red-green

# Use Colour correction to accommodate for colour blindness

Colour blindness affects a large numher of people, and can prove to be a problem when using a phone to browse the web, examine photographs, or generally interact with the user interface.

Thankfully, a built-in accessibility feature can adjust the colour palette of the display to accommodate for colour blindness, making it possible to see tricky colours in a wide range of spectrums. Here's how it works:

**1** Open the **Settings** app and go to **Accessibility** > **Text & Display** > **Colour Correction.**

**2** Toggle **Use colour correction** on. You'll see a preview of the effect in the graphic above.

**3** To fine tune the colour spectrum change, scroll down and select one of the correction modes

# Zoom the entire screen

You can make everything on the screen bigger (or smaller), to help you see text messages, buttons, and other small content. To do this:

**1** Open the **Settings** app and go to **Accessibility** > **Text & Display** > **Display size.**

**2** Use the **slider** at the bottom of the screen to make everything bigger or smaller. As you make changes, you'll see the preview image above change to give you an idea of how large text and content will be.

**3** When you're finished, tap the **back arrow** or close the Settings app to save your changes.

Preview

Large

# Voice Access

Voice Access lets you control your Android device hands-free, by using voice commands to open apps, tap buttons, scroll, type and more. To turn on Voice Access:

1. Open the **Settings** app and go to **Accessibility** > **Voice Access**.

2. Toggle **Use Voice Access** on, then give your device permission to listen to your voice and control the screen.

3. You will then be walked through a tutorial that enables you to customise Voice Access settings.

### Voice Access tips:

- You can tap any words you see on the screen by saying "tap", and then the word you want to tap on.
- If you're unsure about the name or label for something on the screen, say "show labels".
- To type text, select a text box by saying "tap [text box label]", then say "type running five minutes late".
- To see further commands say "help".
- To stop Voice Access from listening, say "stop listening".

Use Voice Access

Options

Voice Access shortcut
Off

Settings

Voice Access lets you control your Android device hands-free. Use voice commands to open apps, tap buttons, scroll, type and more. Currently available in English, French, Italian, German and Spanish only.

---

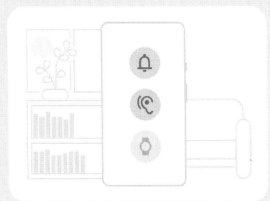

Open Sound notifications

Options

Sound notifications shortcut
Off

# Sound notifications

Sound notifications help you to know what's happening in your home. When activated, this feature will listen for sounds you want to be notified about, such as a smoke alarm or baby crying. It requires you to leave your phone in a separate room and then to receive notifications via a smart watch. If you have a smartwatch connected to your phone, and wish to use this feature, then:

1. Open the **Settings** app and go to **Accessibility** > **Sound notifications**, then tap **Open Sound notifications.**

2. Toggle **Sound notifications** on, and give it permission to record audio.

3. Next, leave your phone in a suitable room and await any notifications on your smartwatch.

# Live Caption

Your phone can automatically detect speech and create captions on the fly. This works when watching videos or even during a phone call. To enable Live Caption:

1. Open the **Settings** app and go to **Accessibility** > **Live Caption**, then toggle **Use Live Caption** on.

2. To customise Live Caption, or to block profanity, scroll down and make your choices using the toggle buttons.

3. Next, begin listening to something with speech, or take a phone call from someone, and watch how captions automatically appear in the middle of the screen.

Live Caption

Use Live Caption

---

Options

Magnification shortcut
Accessibility button

Magnification type
Switch between full and partial screen

m in on the screen

ntent larger.

cut to start magnifi

creen

fingers to move

1. Use shortcut to start magnification
2. Touch & hold anywhere on the screen

# Use magnification

Your Android phone is designed to be easy for anyone to use, even those with visual impairments. However, there might be occasions where you need to zoom into the screen. By using an on-screen magnifying glass, it's possible to examine things in more detail. Here's how it works:

To turn on Magnification, go to **Settings** > **Accessibility** > **Magnification**, then toggle **Magnification shortcut** on. You will then see a magnifying button appear in the lower right corner.

**To zoom in:**
- Tap the **magnifying glass** button, and you'll see a zoomed-in square appear.
- To move the magnifying glass, tap and hold on the button in its bottom right corner, then drag it around the screen.
- To zoom the entire screen, tap the **magnifying glass**, then tap the **full-screen** button which appears afterwards.

# What to do if your phone is full

## Clear storage and RAM...

Your phone only has so much space for storing things like photos, videos and apps. As you take more and more snaps, and install more and more apps, you might reach a point where your phone is completely full and refuses to save anything else.

Similarly, your phone only has a certain amount of memory. Memory (also known as RAM), is used for running multiple things at once, so if you have a lot of apps running in the background you might start to notice apps taking a long time to open, and they might run a little sluggishly too. Here are some helpful tips to enable you to manage these types of problems...

## Free up storage

To tidy up your phone and get back some storage space, open the **Files** app and tap **Clean**. The Files app will then show any suggestions it has found for tidying up your phone. Use these suggestions as you see fit to make more space available.

## Free up memory

If you have an older version of Android, then you can open the **Settings** app, select **Memory**, and see which apps are using the most RAM. You can then close these apps, or uninstall them if they are not necessary.

If you have a newer Android phone, then it's not possible to see which apps are using RAM without installing a third-party app. This is quite a lot of trouble, so instead, open the **Settings** app, select **Apps**, tap **See all [number] apps**, and then uninstall any apps that you don't use on a regular basis. To uninstall an app, select it from the list, then choose **Uninstall**.

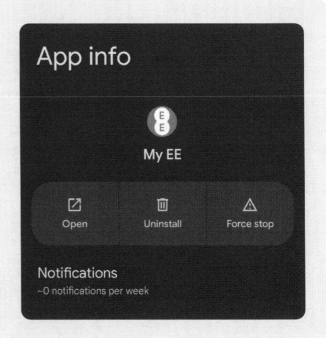

# What to do if you lose your phone

## First of all, don't panic!

It's probably somewhere obvious, like down the side of your sofa or in a jacket pocket. If you've looked around and still can't find it, then it's time to use Find My Device.

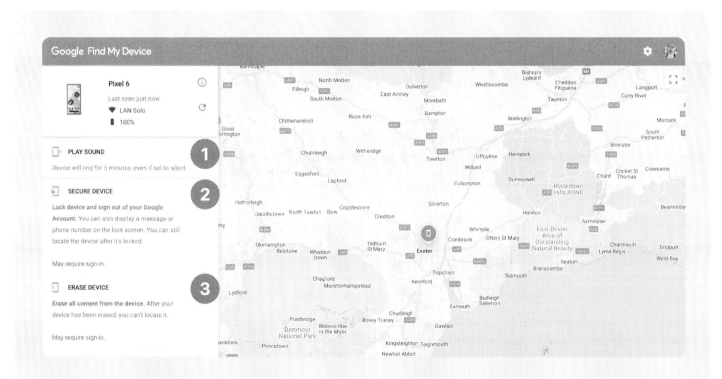

## Use Find My Device

Using Find My Device, you can track all of your Google devices that are logged into your account. You can also ask them to emit a ringing noise, lock them, and even wipe the device so no one can access any of your data.

To log in to Find My Device, either search Google for *"Find my Device"*, or go to **www.google.com/android/find**. Once logged in, you'll see the screen above, where you can select a device and begin to track it down. You'll also see three options:

**1** **Play Sound**
Click this button, and your device will ring for five minutes, even if it's set to silent mode. With luck, you'll be able to quickly track its exact location.

**2** **Secure Device**
Click this button to immediately lock your device and sign out of your Google account. You can also display a message or phone number on the lock screen.

**3** **Erase Device**
If the worst has happened and you don't think you'll be able to get your phone back, then you can securely erase its contents to prevent someone from accessing your data. Note, however, that after your device has been erased, you won't be able to locate or track it anymore.

# Other Problems

## How to quit troublesome apps, or even force your phone to reboot...

It's rare, but sometimes hardware buttons stop responding or become stuck. Perhaps the power button no longer clicks or the volume buttons stop working. If your phone has completely frozen and refuses to respond to taps or hardware buttons, then there are a few things you can try:

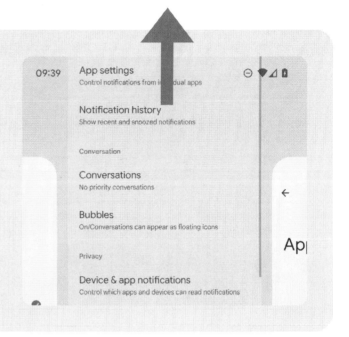

## Force quit an app

- If your smartphone has three icons at the bottom of the screen, tap either the three vertical lines button, or the square button.
- If your smartphone has a single horizontal line at the bottom of the screen, then swipe up from the bottom to the middle of the screen, hold for a moment, then release. You will then see any recently opened apps appear as thumbnails.

To force quit one of these apps, place your finger on the app and then swipe it up and away.

## Force restart your phone

Sometimes your phone might stop responding to touch. This is very rare, but it does happen from time-to-time. In these extreme cases, you can force the device to restart.

To do this, hold both the **power** button and the **volume down** button for up to seven seconds. On older devices, you might have to hold these buttons for up to 20 seconds, so be patient. After a while you'll see the screen go black and the phone will restart itself.

# Drain the battery

In the unlikely event that the screen has stopped responding, *and* the buttons are stuck or broken, then let the battery run dry. Note that this might take up to 10 hours.

# Wi-Fi problems

Wi-Fi connection problems can be a common occurrence. If you're experiencing regular disconnections or slow download speeds, then here are a few things to try:

- Reset the router. Turn it off, wait for 10 seconds to clear its cache, then power it back on.

- Get closer to the router. Thick concrete walls can sometimes block the connection.

- Reconnect. To do this go to **Settings** > **Network and Internet**, tap on the network, choose **Disconnect**, then try to reconnect to the same network.

# Phone not charging

If your device isn't charging then there a couple of things you can try:

- Leave it plugged in. If the battery is fully drained, then it can take up to 20 minutes for it to start charging.

- Blow air into the charge port. Dust or pocket flint might have worked its way into the port. A can of compressed air is your best option.

# Phone not powering on

If you've followed the previous step and left the device plugged in for at least 20 minutes, then something serious is likely to be happening. Your best bet is to take it into a phone repair shop, explain the problem, then leave it to the experts.

# Index

# Stay inspired

## Beginners Guides:

**Beginners Guide
to iPad**

**978-1-914347-94-8**

$19.75 USA
$22.99 CAN
£10.99 UK
$22.99 AUD

**Beginners Guide
to Mac**

**978-1-914347-93-1**

$19.75 USA
$22.99 CAN
£10.99 UK
$22.99 AUD

## Ultimate Guides:

**iPad:
Ultimate Guide**

**978-1-914347-07-8**

$19.75 USA
$22.99 CAN
£10.99 UK
$22.99 AUD

**MacBook:
Ultimate Guide**

**978-1-914347-08-5**

$19.75 USA
$22.99 CAN
£10.99 UK
$22.99 AUD

**iPhone 13:
Ultimate Guide**

**978-1-914347-96-2**

$19.75 USA
$22.99 CAN
£10.99 UK
$22.99 AUD

## Other Guides:

**iPhone 12 Guide**

**979-8699016419**

$12.98 USA
$14.98 CAN
£9.98 UK

**iPad Pro Guide**

**979-8651084746**

$12.98 USA
$14.98 CAN
£9.98 UK

**iMac Guide**

**979-8699016419**

$12.98 USA
$14.98 CAN
£9.98 UK

**Tesla Ultimate
Guide**

**978-1-914347-04-7**

$19.75 USA
$22.99 CAN
£10.99 UK
$22.99 AUD

**Alexa Complete
Guide**

**978-1-914347-03-0**

$12.98 USA
$14.98 CAN
£9.98 UK

## Visit www.leafpublishing.co.uk to find out more

Made in United States
Troutdale, OR
01/28/2024

17245432R00091